AQA GCSE
English

Skills for Language & Literature

Philip Allan Updates, an imprint of Hodder Education, an Hachette UK company, Market Place, Deddington, Oxfordshire OX15 0SE

Orders

Bookpoint Ltd, 130 Milton Park, Abingdon, Oxfordshire OX14 4SB

tel: 01235 827720

fax: 01235 400454

e-mail: uk.orders@bookpoint.co.uk

Lines are open 9.00 a.m.–5.00 p.m., Monday to Saturday, with a 24-hour message answering service.

You can also order through the Philip Allan Updates website: www.philipallan.co.uk

© Philip Allan Updates 2010

ISBN 978-1-4441-0874-3

First printed 2010

Impression number 5 4 3 2 1

Year 2015 2014 2013 2012 2011 2010

Printed in Italy

Hachette UK's policy is to use papers that are natural, renewable and recyclable products and made from wood grown in sustainable forests. The logging and manufacturing processes are expected to conform to the environmental regulations of the country of origin.

P01682

Contents

Introduction

There are plenty of GCSE English textbooks on the market, so what makes this one any different?

First, this textbook is written by three highly experienced teachers and examiners who have many years of experience in different types of schools. We have pooled our experience to make sure this is not only an interesting and engaging read but, most importantly, a foundation for exam success.

Second, this book provides a different way of approaching GCSE English by focusing on the Assessment Objectives upon which the AQA GCSE English course is based. It is a skills-based course book which recognises the fact that there is little or no content in English and English Literature.

However, because this book is based on Assessment Objectives, it can be used for any examination board. The AOs in speaking and listening, reading and writing are the same for every board, so students and teachers can use this book whatever summative assessment they are aiming for. This book equips students with the skills for success and is not tied to specific examinations or controlled conditions tasks. Teachers may wish to focus on one discrete component, like reading, or integrate aspects from each section, especially the use of speaking and listening as a fundamental means for students to arrive at their own meanings and to learn, rather than be taught.

Third, the integral use of examiner comments on sample student work gives you an unprecedented view into the mind of an examiner. This will not only help you to make sense of the world of examining and assessment, but allow you to assess yourself (known as Assessment for Learning in modern educational parlance) and to see the clear links between one grade and the next.

Finally, this book is different from other textbooks in terms of its structure. Its first three sections cover the portable skills of reading, writing, and speaking and listening. For this reason, although this is mainly a GCSE English textbook, it reinforces the links between the reading and writing Assessment Objectives, wherever they may be assessed. You must find evidence to back up your explanations in controlled conditions work and the exam papers, so it makes sense to focus on the portable skill rather than the content. This explains the inclusion of a chapter that focuses on the broad skills needed to respond to a range of literary techniques used by writers in literature rather than discussing each of the different poems and novels in turn.

There is a glossary of terms at the end of the book. You do not gain marks for knowing terms at GCSE, but you do need to understand them in order to attain the Assessment Objectives. The glossary explains some basic terms you should know.

The next two pages show you the special features of this book and how to use them. So, get started and boost your grade by taking the advice of the experts!

John Nield
Graham Fletcher
Unsah Tabassum

Also available from the same authors:

AQA GCSE English: Skills for Language & Literature Teacher Guide + CD
(978-1-4441-0875-0)

Included within this guide is a CD-ROM with all the audio material to support the speaking and listening activities in this textbook. The Teacher Guide also contains: skills teaching map, activities with teacher notes, worksheets and answers, photocopiable planning grids, assessment advice and PowerPoints.

AQA GCSE English: Skills for Achieving an A*
(978-1-4441-1081-4)

A student book aimed at developing higher level skills in reading, writing, speaking and listening which explores the advanced skills need for higher-level exam success.

How to use this book

Student responses: sample answers to the set tasks.

Assessment for Learning: activities that allow students to practise their skills in solo and group work.

How to improve: advice from the examiner on how student responses could be improved to achieve more marks.

Examiner's comments: these highlight the good and bad points of student responses.

Highlighting: coloured highlighting links the examiner's comments to the student responses, showing what is required to gain marks.

Remember boxes: these are used throughout the book to remind you of exactly what the examiners are looking for.

Section A | Reading

the magazine is presented. He makes a point (P), finds a relevant example (E) and gives an explanation (E). This shows that the material has been selected and arranged to fit the answer.

How to improve

Do not waste time and effort writing a long introduction that simply restates the question. The first sentence of this answer is pointless because it just repeats the words of the task.

Student answer 3

In my opinion, this front page of a middle-of-the-road magazine is a mess. It is very bitty and it almost puts the reader off with its dog's dinner of presentational devices that do not really complement each other.

First, the most successful aspect of the front page is the use of images, which clearly attract the reader's attention by their appeal to the target audience. There is not simply any image of a woman: the main image is one that most of the readers of this magazine would aspire to. This is a successful presentational device on a few different levels.

Second, the straplines at the bottom of the page offer readers a mixture of emotions and story-lines. The four images all contain faces (or an X-rayed hand!) in an obvious attempt to appeal to the female target audience. But who would offer such stories for publication? These stories are linked to other stories on the front page by the garishly coloured backgrounds which are contrasted with the baby blue next to the baby. Once more, the use of these 'girlie' colours is almost condescending. Finally, we come to the puff at the top right-hand side of the page. It is garishly coloured in the ubiquitous red and yellow seen elsewhere. Both the presentation and the implicit horror of this story about a 2st cyst, with an accompanying picture, would attract prospective readers to buy the magazine.

I think the presentation of this page is very poor. It fulfils its role of trying to sell more copies of the magazine, but it fails to present a front page which successfully advertises what is on offer inside its pages.

Examiner's comment

This answer would gain an A grade, not because it is longer but because it shows that the student has absorbed the material and shaped it to fit the question. Notice that, like the F-grade candidate, this student spotted the main image, but instead of simply describing it she has commented on how the magazine uses it. The skills required to earn a Grade A include:

- clear and detailed understanding of what the question is asking
- careful and logical argument, backed up with examples
- material fully absorbed and shaped for purpose
- sophisticated and convincing use of technical terminology to describe media concepts

---

Assessment Objectives for reading | **1**

How to improve

Use technical terminology convincingly and in a way that is helpful, as a sort of shorthand. For example, the words 'strapline' and 'puff' used in this answer are recognised terms in journalism.

Assessment for learning

What skills do you think are demonstrated by each of the highlighted examples in the final answer? Discuss them with a partner and explain how they exemplify the Grade A descriptors above.

Remember: all candidates should be able to spot material; the better ones are able to evaluate it.

Combining AO2(i) and AO2(iii)

You may be asked to compare, or make cross-references between, the use of presentational devices in the English or English Language examination.

How is this assessed

This is usually assessed if you are required to read two or more items on the same subject, or if they use devices in similar or different ways.

We have already compared two texts for understanding, AO2(i) on pages 8–9, but we are now going to start to put the Assessment Objectives together and compare the uses of linguistic/grammatical, structural and presentational features, AO2(iii).

Grade A	A complete answer which compares all parts of the question equally well.
Grade C	A clear and structured attempt to compare.
Grade F	An unstructured attempt to compare, but tends to identify features.

Parts of these three basic grade descriptors should now be beginning to sound familiar.

How can you improve your answers?

To gain a grade higher than a D you have to make a clear comparison, finding either a similarity, a difference, or both. To make your comparisons clear you should continue to use words and phrases such as those in the table on page 8.

Remember: you can also use comparatives such as **bigger, louder, brighter, more colourful** and **clearer**. It is a good idea to compare things which are similar or different in obvious ways too.

Key words: a student-friendly decoder of terms used in the Assessment Objectives.

Ladder of skills: these boxes show how the Assessment Objectives are assessed at different grades.

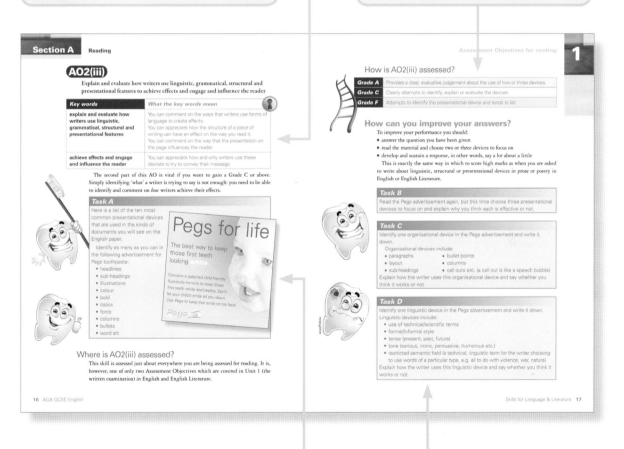

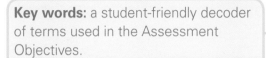

Tasks: these are provided throughout the book to encourage you to apply the skills you need in order to do well.

Chapter 1

Assessment Objectives for reading

Why does reading amount to 40% of the marks for GCSE English? The answer is found in what examiners are required to assess.

Under the topic of reading you must show that you can read with understanding, select appropriate material from different sources and comment on language, presentation and grammar. The big difference with this new specification is that you have to write a lot about a little. In other words, there is much more to reading than simply casting your eyes over pages of print. On occasions, your ability as a reader can be assessed orally, but the main way your reading will be tested is through your writing. To read successfully for the examination and controlled assessments, you must learn how to write about what you read.

What are you required to read? First, you must read some literature, regardless of whether or not you are entering the English Literature examination. Some is set for controlled conditions under the guidance of your teacher, but you also need to study texts from different cultures. Second, you have to study some non-fiction, including media texts, for the written examination.

For GCSE English, your reading will be assessed against the following Assessment Objectives (AOs). The English Literature AOs are printed underneath the English AOs in blue.

AO2(i)	• **Read and understand texts**, **selecting material appropriate to purpose**, **collating different sources** and making **comparisons** and **cross-references** where appropriate.
AO1	• Respond to texts critically and imaginatively; select and evaluate relevant textual detail to illustrate and support interpretations.
AO3	• Make comparisons and explain links between texts, evaluating writers' different ways of expressing meaning and achieving effects.
AO2(ii)	• **Develop** and **sustain** interpretations of **writers' ideas** and **perspectives**.
AO2(iii)	• **Explain** and **evaluate** how writers use **linguistic**, **grammatical**, **structural** and **presentational** features to **achieve effects** and **engage** and **influence** the reader.
AO2	• Explain how language, structure and form contribute to writers' presentation of ideas, themes and settings.
AO2(iv)	• **Understand** texts in their **social**, **cultural** and **historical** contexts.
AO4	• Relate texts to their social, cultural and historical contexts; explain how texts have been influential and significant to self and other readers in different contexts and at different times.

English and English Literature mostly share the same AOs, so we will refer to the English AOs in the main, other than where there is a noteworthy difference.

Read and understand texts, selecting material appropriate to purpose, collating different sources and making comparisons and cross-references where appropriate

Key words	What the key words mean
read and understand texts	You read a text and work out what it means for you.
selecting material appropriate to purpose	You should choose the relevant parts of the text to support your comments.
collating different sources and making comparisons and cross-references	You develop a series of connected comments about two or more texts, finding similarities and differences.

Where is AO2(i) assessed?

This AO is assessed just about everywhere you are being assessed for reading: it is the fundamental test of whether you can read and understand.

How is AO2(i) assessed?

This is usually assessed if you are required to read a single item, or two or more items on the same subject. It is possible to make comparisons within the same text, but it is more usual to be asked to look at two different texts.

Grade A	A personal and persuasive response which looks at how details can inform meaning, choosing apt quotations and making telling comparisons and cross-references.
Grade C	A clear and structured attempt to engage, referring to specific aspects of texts with clear evidence of comparison and cross-reference.
Grade F	Main ideas and arguments are described with reference to specific aspects or details to justify a view with simple comparisons.

In order to gain a Grade C or above against this Assessment Objective you need to think about what it means in practice.

- You must understand the basic content: what the words and sentences mean literally.
- You must be able to use evidence from the text to support what you think it means. A text has no meaning until you read it, but you have to back up what you say by referring to the text directly (by quotations) or indirectly (by references).
- You must interpret, or 'read between the lines', to understand the real meaning of the words. When we are dealing purely with the written word, we must always look beyond the simple, basic meaning. We must look for clues that the writer may include for us.

> **Remember:** when you are reading, you must decide what you think the writer is trying to say and what evidence you can supply to back up your view.

Reading and understanding texts

Reading and understanding a text requires the same skills whatever reading task you are doing, whether it is for controlled conditions or external examination. You need to consider:

- What is the main point that the writer is making?
- What are the minor points and how do they connect with the main point? You need to look at the details and see how they connect with each other.

This is only formally assessed under examination conditions in Unit 1, but you need to show evidence of this skill whenever you read any text-based part of your English course.

TAJ/Fotolia

Task A

Read the passage on diet below. What argument is being put forward in it?

Rubbish in leads to rubbish out

Government experts are blaming some of schoolchildren's bad behaviour on unhealthy school meals.

Most school dinners contain a lot of the foods linked to poor behaviour, but they also lack minerals that help to keep children emotionally balanced. One research group found that a primary school child eating five school dinners a week consumed 40% more salt, 28% more saturated fat and 20% more sugar than recommended levels.

Chocolate + sugar = trouble

Dr Neil Ward from Surrey University said that too much sugar and chocolate and not enough zinc and iron were linked to bad behaviour. Many experts believe that better diets could lead to fewer children being diagnosed with ADHD and needing drugs like Ritalin.

A Mars a day helps you…?

International studies showed that changing the diets of young offenders could reduce antisocial behaviour by 61% without side effects. In one institution, this was a simple matter of reducing the amount of sugar, chocolate, biscuits and fizzy drinks and giving mineral supplements. Dr Ward said, 'The governor said he could not believe we had taken a young man, who was inside for killing both his parents and who was constantly aggressive, and made him human.'

Student response to Task A

Student answer 1

Government experts blame bad behaviour on unhealthy school meals. School dinners contain 40% too much salt, 28% too much fat and 20% too much sugar. Dr Neil Ward also says that children eat too much chocolate.

Examiner's comment

This candidate has simply copied from the original text and hardly changed the author's words. She has concentrated on the opening part of the article, so has not followed the whole argument. The examiner cannot tell if the candidate has understood the text. The answer would receive a Grade F or below.

How to improve

'Select material': use parts of the original text to support your answer, do not simply copy it out.

Student answer 2

Government experts say that school dinners can lead to poor behaviour and that children are eating too much of the wrong sort of food. Dr Ward says that too much sugar and chocolate are particularly bad and that better diets can lead to better behaviour. International studies have also shown how the behaviour of aggressive young men can be improved by changing diet.

Examiner's comment

This is a good example of a candidate who answers the question by looking at the whole argument. Although some of the writer's original words have been kept, there is clear use of the candidate's own words too. This candidate tries to sum up the whole argument by making a general point in the last sentence. He would be awarded a Grade C.

How to improve

Go into more detail and try to generalise more about what you think the writer is really saying.

Student answer 3

The writer of this article set out to show how poor the diet of today's schoolchildren is and to show how changes can make a massive difference to performance and behaviour. He points to the poor nature of the food given to schoolchildren at lunchtime and argues that big improvements can be made by making quite simple changes. These changes to diet can also make big differences to young offenders.

Examiner's comment

This candidate has read the article, then asked what argument the writer wanted to get across to the reader. She has stood back from the article and has not just paraphrased it. For example, instead of simply referring to school dinners, the candidate has referred to diet. She appreciates that the article is not really about schools or young offenders but about the effects of diet and nutrition on the young.

Note that the candidate has written about the same number of words as the previous student, but grasps the whole argument, not just the individual details. She would gain a Grade A.

How to improve

Practise developing this skill whenever you are asked to read.

Look at the two texts on pages 6 and 8: 'Possible punk princess?' and 'A music fan's blog'. Both passages are about the same person, but they have different views.

Task B

Read the article entitled 'Possible punk princess?' (on the next page).
What does the writer of this article think about:
- Sabine Lebrun as a person?
- Sabine Lebrun as a pop star?

Remember: there are two parts to this question in addition to the actual reading.

Pop Report, Spring 2009

Possible punk princess?

Laura Stretton went to see Canadian punk rocker Sabine Lebrun punching and pouting on her latest concert tour, and wonders if she is next in line for the pop-punk throne

Canadian pop regularly produces arena-filling pop stars who can make a lot of noise, without really saying very much. I can think of Bryan Adams, Celine Dion and Alanis Morissette. Sabine Lebrun (note the typically French Canadian name) is currently out-shouting all of them. Even before this leg of her tour, she has sold a massive 12m copies of her debut album *Je Suis*.

This is middle-of-the-road pop music with a punk twist which this crowd loved last night at the Manchester Arcade. The punk rock twist is a power-ful selling point as I see Sabine look-alikes starting at the age of 10 and finishing at the age of 45 at this concert, where they are all very obviously enjoying themselves. Lebrun herself is dressed in pink fishnet tights, but she sounds more like the Sugar Babes than any former punk heroes.

Lebrun does not do a lot on stage apart from punch the air and carry a guitar around which she occasionally strums. However, her voice is very powerful and that is her biggest plus point. And, just like other punk rock stars, she looks really negative and depressed most of the time. She sings about being 'weird' while drinking bottled water and looks like she has used a whole bottle of eye-liner to make herself look so good. (I wonder what she looks like without it?)

There are reports in the pop press about her strict childhood and the attitude of her parents towards her success. But does Sabine mind as she bounces into her next single *Bad Attitude*, which is bound to be another hit?

In a brisk hour on stage, she keeps to her script very carefully, except when an oaf of a fan is invited onto the stage and she appears to really enjoy the fun that they are having. During the line 'You look a fool to me' she mimes a kick at him and it brings the loudest cheer of the night. If nothing else, this last show of tomboy foolery suggests that Sabine Lebrun has a lot more character to show.

Maybe she will become pop-punk's pouting princess and then become the queen when Madonna gives up her throne. Maybe. I enjoyed this.

See more of Sabine Lebrun at Brixton Arcade, London SW9 from tonight until Thursday of this week. Box office open until late.

Assessment for Learning

1 What are your first impressions of Sabine? What do you think of her attitudes?
2 Write down three words/phrases that show her attitudes.
3 Now compare your words with a partner's and discuss what is similar and different and why.
4 Have you changed your mind about anything?

Student response to Task B

I don't think that the writer really likes Sabine Lebrun because she plays 'middle of the road pop music' but she did enjoy the concert because she says 'I enjoyed this'. She thinks that Sabine is a bit of a loudmouth because she shouted a lot during her performance. Also she thought Sabine looked depressed.

Examiner's comment

The main ideas from the article are expressed and specific aspects of the argument are used to give examples and to back up the student's response. If you read the F descriptors on page 3, this would just about fulfil all of them.

How to improve

Be more impersonal and try to engage with the whole text.

Assessment for Learning

Identify three things that this student has done really well and two things that could have been better. Discuss your findings with a partner.

Task C

Write a C-grade response to the question, copying out and using the following frame to structure your answer. (Although frames are restrictive, they give you the initial structure within which you can develop your own ideas. You will soon find that you have no need for such rigid support.)

What does the writer of this article think about: Sabine Lebrun as a person?	What does the writer of this article think about: Sabine Lebrun as a pop star?
1 Because…	1 Because…

Assessment for Learning

Exchange your work with another student and assess whether you think that theirs is a 'clear and structured' answer. It will probably be structured because of the frame, but is it a clear answer to the question?

How can you improve your answers?

To gain a Grade C or above, you need to answer the questions that you are set, giving evidence for your views and finding either a similarity, a difference, or both *if you are asked to do so.*

To make your comparisons clear you should learn how to use words and phrases such as those in the table below. You can also use comparatives such as **bigger**, **louder**, **brighter**, **more colourful** and **clearer**.

Showing similarities			
like	also	the same as	as
comparable to	corresponding to	too	resembles
both	similarly	likewise	in the same way

Showing differences			
but	however	in comparison with	conversely
on the other hand	contrasting with	unlike	whereas
nevertheless	although	except	yet

Task D

Read the following blog by a music fan who attended the concert at the Arcade, Manchester, given by Sabine Lebrun. What is this blogger's opinion of the concert review? Explain:

- how it changes your opinion of the original review
- how they are similar and different

Remember: there are three parts to this question in addition to the actual reading: one 'what' and two 'hows'.

SEARCH BLOG ⚑ FLAG BLOG SHARE Next Blog»

uBlog

A music fan's blog
Awesome!!!!!!!!!! I have never enjoyed a gig so much in my life. Hate to comment here- but cant help but feel like the review in the paper didn't do it justice. As if to say "Sabine isnt a true punk rocker, so she's lightweight" OR 'I'm the only one who gets it..I know what it's all about...the music...unlike you teenagers." or like "we were there when the Sex Pistols wrecked the place". The snobishness shines through in the whole article. Its well known that Sabine doesn't do drugs and that but she doesn't need to when her music is so good and her voice is so strong. By the way, my friend was the 'oaf of a fan' and he will remember this gig for the rest of his life. And what was all that about at the end 'I enjoyed this!' Sure you did grandad.

Terry Strickland

Remember: this is a blog and is not grammatically correct.

Student response to Task D

This blogger obviously enjoyed the whole concert, even the part that so annoyed the original reviewer, when the 'oaf of a fan' was on stage. The adjective that starts the blog clearly gives his view and the number of exclamation marks suggests a true fanatic. Unsurprisingly, the blogger was not impressed by the review because the reviewer seems to have a very negative view about Lebrun's abilities as both a singer and a performer. The reviewer begins by suggesting that Lebrun comes from a long line of Canadian shouters and that she can out-shout all of them. Hardly an auspicious start!

However, it is the lack of supposed punk credentials that the blogger most takes exception to. The blogger no longer directly refers to the original review, but picks up on the perceived criticism of Lebrun as light-weight because, although she was suitably dressed and depressed, she does not have any of the self-destructive attributes of the Sex Pistols et al.

Finally, the blogger can hold himself in no longer and accuses the reviewer of being 'a grandad', the most telling criticism of anyone who wishes to be involved with youth culture.

How does this change my opinion of the original review? Not a lot really. I have not got the same fanatical baggage as the blogger and I quite enjoyed the critical stance taken by Laura Stretton.

They are certainly very different in many respects. The review is critical in the true sense of the word. Stretton finds both good and bad to say about Lebrun's performance, but there is an almost apologetic 'I enjoyed this.' at the very end. Maybe she realised that she was being a little too critical and the backers of the concert may not advertise in her newspaper any more. However, the biggest difference is in the evidence that they both use to support their views. While Stretton seems to refer to a thorough knowledge of the music industry with her references to other Canadian singers, Strickland descends to personal jibes, putting words into Stretton's mouth in a very juvenile way.

Examiner's comment

This is a clear and structured answer, but it is a bit uneven. The structure shows that the student was confident with the first 'what' part of the question but wrote less about the two 'how' parts of the question. However, length is not always a good measure and the answer does show some of the qualities of a higher-grade response. In the first paragraph, two of the many details that the student picks up on are highlighted.

There are also several comparisons. These are not always apt, but they are numerous. The words and phrases which suggest comparison have been highlighted in the last paragraph.

This is certainly a 'personal and persuasive' response that is tentative and willing to suggest that there may be alternative interpretations. The student is also beginning to show clear evidence of being able to say a lot about a little, or to 'develop and sustain interpretations of writers' ideas and perspectives.'

> **How to improve**
>
> Focus clearly on the task in hand and always write a short plan when comparing so that you make valid comparisons.

AO2(ii)

Develop and sustain interpretations of writers' ideas and perspectives

Key words	What the key words mean
develop and sustain interpretations	Write a lot about a little. You are expected to 'go on about', or expand upon details in order to show different interpretations of writers' ideas or concepts.
writers' ideas and perspectives	These are what writers were hoping to convey when they started writing the texts.

Where is AO2(ii) assessed?

Once more, this AO is assessed just about everywhere you are being assessed for reading, especially in English Literature. The controlled assessment tasks in particular give you the opportunity to go into detail on your chosen aspects. A typical controlled assessment task for GCSE English Literature Unit 3: the significance of Shakespeare and the English Literary Heritage is given in Section D (see pages 145–47).

How is AO2(ii) assessed?

This is a key descriptor for differentiating between a C-grade candidate and the higher grades of B, A and A*. Writers at the higher levels of performance do not simply state the obvious answer, they go beyond the obvious and even write about apparently contradictory ideas and perspectives. They will use phrases like: 'the writer could also be saying…'; 'in addition he may be trying to…'; 'on the other hand, she may be…'.

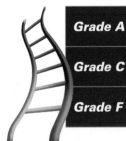

Grade A	Responds to a variety of texts, developing how details engage and affect the reader and discussing writers' perspectives.
Grade C	Shows understanding by selecting and commenting on how specific aspects can achieve different effects.
Grade F	Deals with and describes the main ideas in a text and makes simple, but specific comments.

How can you improve your answers?

You should ask yourself the following questions when writing your responses:

- So what?
- What else might the writer be saying?

• Could there be an alternative meaning or perspective?
• How am I going to back up my views?

This section looks at how you can develop and sustain your answer (write a lot about a little) by looking at how facts and opinions are used in two advertisements for Delillo© boots. The different responses to these questions show how 'developing and sustaining a response' can improve your grade.

> **Remember:** identifying and explaining about fact and opinion is just another way of showing that you can: 'Read and understand texts, selecting material appropriate to purpose, collating different sources' (AO2i).

Task A

Read the advertisement for girls' football boots, then answer the following questions:

1 Identify one fact and one opinion from the advert and write them down.

2 Explain how the writer uses this fact and this opinion.

Note: Question 1 is a typical Foundation Tier question in that it really only tests lower-level reading skills. Therefore the answer will simply *identify*. Question 2 asks for an explanation. This is the sort of skill, if you can prove clearly that you have it, which will indicate to your teacher that you have Higher Tier reading skills.

Bury it like Becca!
These boots are made for scoring

Delillo© boots have long been associated with the best in women's soccer. Now we've developed the ultimate boot with you in mind.

The obvious choice of internationals on both sides of the Atlantic, *Delillo©* boots are made for the discerning woman footballer:

✓ soft-touch kangaroo leather gives you the sort of control you want

✓ full leather fold-over tongue gives you the comfort you need

✓ 8 removable studs give you the sort of grip you demand

Here are some views from top players:

'I was unconvinced until I scored that equaliser in last year's final. They are a brilliant boot with plenty of grip and colour that I like.'
Trudy Ulthorp

'I've buried hundreds of goals in my career, but these allow me to bury more balls in the back of the net than ever.'
Becca Gamble, England Captain

So, if you want to bury them like Becca, get down to your local sports shop where you will receive a personalised fitting and advice on after-care. After all, if boots are worth buying, they're worth looking after.

Delillo©
a lifetime of sport

Task B

Answer the same questions for the Delillo© B-line Series 2006 advertisement.

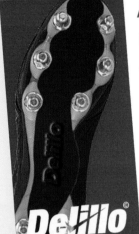

Delillo B-line Series 2006

As worn by the Everton under-16 squad

Winners of the under-16 Charity Shield 2004/05

Are your boots past their best? Are they an embarrassment in the changing room? Then make a beeline for your nearest stockist and buy a pair of Delillo B-line boots.

Delillo B-line Series is available in sizes 5–11 (inc. ½ sizes), 12 and 13. For young players who want a responsive boot with a sleek, sock-like fit. The boot has a Struction outer covering for excellent grip on all types of natural surfaces and comes in two exciting new colours.

Our price only **£28**.99
(ref. DEL1220)

Task C

1 Compare how the two advertisements use facts and opinions.
2 In what ways are they similar and in what ways do they differ?

Student response to Task A

1 A fact is that they have eight removable studs. An opinion is that Delillo has 'long been associated with the best in women's soccer'.
2 I know the first one is a fact because you can prove it by counting the number of studs. The second one is an opinion because there is no way of knowing if it is true or not.

Examiner's comment

The candidate answers the first question correctly. Facts tend to lurk close to numbers, and opinions cannot be proved. How do we know that Delillo has this sort of historical link? However, the candidate does not answer the second question. He is explaining why each is a fact or opinion rather than explaining how they are used.

How to improve

Never simply identify a device: always explain how it is being used if this is required by the question.

Student response to Task B

This advertisement for Delillo B-line Series football boots uses the fact that they were worn by the under-16 Charity Shield winning Everton side because some people will be impressed if this side wore them. It is, however, an opinion that the two new colours are 'exciting'. The writers of this advert use these words because they know that purchasers are impressed by positive sounding adjectives like 'new' and 'exciting'.

Examiner's comment

This student clearly answers Task B, by explaining why she thinks her choices of fact and opinion have been used. Her reasons are valid, so this response would earn a Grade C.

How to improve

Go into more detail with reasons. There may even be apparently contradictory reasons why a device may be used.

Student response to Task C

The two advertisements use facts for very similar reasons: they both use them to give positive views of the boots they are selling and to give information. The first advert quotes three bulleted facts which are intermingled with opinions. These facts are used in the same way as the second advert uses facts about materials and price, to inform the reader.

Similarly, because they are both promotional adverts, the writers use opinions for broadly similar reasons. They use adjectives to give biased and opinionated views about their products. In the first advert words like 'ultimate', 'obvious' and 'discerning' are used, while the second advert uses similarly biased adjectives, such as 'excellent' and 'exciting' in order to influence the reader's choice.

Examiner's comment

This is the best of the three responses for several reasons:

- The student has clearly answered the question by using the comparison and structuring words.
- There is some detail in this answer and the student has clearly developed and sustained the answer.
- Short quotations are embedded in the answer.
- The student uses sophisticated vocabulary, such as 'biased', which helps to conceptualise the response.

How to improve

Go into even greater depth with explanations, especially when, and if, asked about writer's intentions.

This Assessment Objective is just as important when reading poetry, or any other form of literature. For example, the poem included below can have lots of meanings: your task is to come up with your own understanding and to back up your views with references to the poem. Even if you are not studying English Literature, you need to be able to apply your skills as a reader as identified in the Assessment Objectives to whatever you read, including poetry.

The poem we are going to look at is not one of the poems from the English Literary Heritage. Poets that you could read for this piece of controlled conditions work for English or English Literature include the following pre-twentieth-century poets:

Blake   Coleridge   Donne   **Keats**   **Tennyson**   Wordsworth

and the following twentieth-century poets:

Frost   **Heaney**   Hughes   Owen   Plath   **Yeats**

Task D

Read the following poem and explain what you think the poet is trying to convey (his conceptualisation) by referring to the poem whenever, and wherever, possible.

Chidiock Tichborne's Elegy
written with his own hand in the Tower before his execution

My prime of youth is but a frost of cares,
My feast of joy is but a dish of pain,
My crop of corn is but a field of tares,
And all my good is but vain hope of gain.
The day is past, and yet I saw no sun,
And now I live, and now my life is done.

My tale was heard and yet it was not told,
My fruit is fallen and yet my leaves are green;
My youth is spent and yet I am not old,
I saw the world and yet I was not seen.
My thread is cut and yet it is not spun,
And now I live, and now my life is done.

I sought my death and found it in my womb,
I looked for life and saw it was a shade;
I trod the earth and knew it was my tomb,
And now I die, and now I was but made.
My glass is full, and now my glass is run,
And now I live, and now my life is done.

1586

> **Remember:** this is a higher-order reading skill and goes beyond literal meaning to implied and tentative ideas: your ideas and what you think the writer's may be. We can no longer ask the poet because he is dead, but we can have our own ideas so long as they can be supported by reference to the text.

Student response to Task D

I think that this poet is very annoyed by the fact that he is going to die before his time and I am going to refer to the last line of each stanza to justify my view. As the last line is repeated three times, it can be looked upon as a rhetorical device: the poet is attempting to draw attention to his plight by repeating the paradoxical statement:

'And now I live, and now my life is done.'

There are three different ways in which I want to look at this line: its literal meaning, its importance structurally and its linguistic significance. First, it is

Ivan Tsurkan/Fotolia

pretty obvious that it means that although he is still breathing, his life in the Tower is as good as over as he awaits his execution. He is in a state of limbo as he lists all of the ways that he has not fulfilled his potential, but he writes: 'I sought my death and found it in my womb,' which is an odd thing for a man to say. However, I believe that he means that he was doomed to die from his very birth; from his mother's womb. This could have been because of some religious persecution (Catholicism?), or some other reason that would have made him unpopular with the establishment.

The line is important structurally because it not only forms a conclusion to each stanza, but it also does so in a very definite way: the word 'done' is very definite and makes the end of each stanza even more end-stopped, just like his life is going to be end-stopped. This aspect obviously leads me on to its linguistic significance. The full stop at the end of each stanza reinforces the inevitability of the end, but it may also be partly custom, because this is what poets did at the end of stanzas at this time in the seventeenth century. This custom does not, however, take away from the power of the line in my opinion.

Perhaps most interestingly, each of these last lines is an oxymoron which sort of sums up the nature of the poet's life. The linguistic structure of the line reinforces the meaning, with the comma almost acting like a fulcrum of meaning in each case. Each of the words in these lines is very simple and seems to add to the inevitability of the situation he finds himself in. This inevitability is also reinforced by the rhythm of every line, which is like a heart beat: and this poet's heart is going to stop beating soon. Good line, isn't it?

Examiner's comment

The word 'wow' does not appear in any mark scheme, but maybe it should: 'wow!' This response has everything you would want in an A* answer. There is plenty of evidence of this student 'developing how details engage and affect the reader and discussing writers' perspectives'.

How to improve

Become your class expert so that you can share your ideas and help others to learn.

Assessment for Learning

1 Read through this answer as if you were an examiner and identify where there is clear evidence of the following skills:
   - focus on detail
   - willingness to suggest different responses
   - willingness to give a personal view
   - use of evidence to support views
   - writing a lot about a little
2 Discuss your findings with a partner in preparation for a class discussion.
3 Discuss whether this answer could have been improved in any way, or any ways that you differ from this student's views.

AO2(iii)

Explain and evaluate how writers use linguistic, grammatical, structural and presentational features to achieve effects and engage and influence the reader

Key words	What the key words mean
explain and evaluate how writers use linguistic, grammatical, structural and presentational features	You can comment on the ways that writers use forms of language to create effects. You can appreciate how the structure of a piece of writing can have an effect on the way you read it. You can comment on the way that the presentation on the page influences the reader.
achieve effects and engage and influence the reader	You can appreciate how and why writers use these devices to try to convey their message.

The second part of this AO is vital if you want to gain a Grade C or above. Simply identifying 'what' a writer is trying to say is not enough: you need to be able to identify and comment on *how* writers achieve their effects.

Task A

Here is a list of the ten most common presentational devices that are used in the kinds of documents you will see on the English paper.

Identify as many as you can in the following advertisement for Pegs toothpaste:

- headlines
- sub-headings
- illustrations
- colour
- bold
- italics
- fonts
- columns
- bullets
- word art

Pegs for life

The best way to keep those first teeth looking white

Contains a patented child-friendly fluoroxide formula to keep those first teeth white and healthy. Don't let your child's smile let you down. Use *Pegs* to keep that smile on his face!

Where is AO2(iii) assessed?

This skill is assessed just about everywhere you are being assessed for reading. It is, however, one of only two Assessment Objectives which are covered in Unit 1 (the written examination) in English and English Literature.

How is AO2(iii) assessed?

Grade A	Provides a clear, evaluative judgement about the use of two or three devices.
Grade C	Clearly attempts to identify, explain or evaluate the devices.
Grade F	Attempts to identify the presentational device and tends to list.

How can you improve your answers?

To improve your performance you should:

- answer the question you have been given
- read the material and choose two or three devices to focus on
- develop and sustain a response, in other words, say a lot about a little

This is exactly the same way in which to score high marks as when you are asked to write about linguistic, structural or presentational devices in prose or poetry in English or English Literature.

Task B

Read the Pegs advertisement again, but this time choose three presentational devices to focus on and explain why you think each is effective or not.

Task C

Identify one organisational device in the Pegs advertisement and write it down.

Organisational devices include:

- paragraphs
- layout
- sub-headings
- bullet points
- columns
- call outs etc. (a call out is like a speech bubble)

Explain how the writer uses this organisational device and say whether you think it works or not.

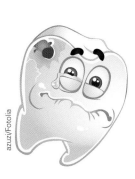

Task D

Identify one linguistic device in the Pegs advertisement and write it down. Linguistic devices include:

- use of technical/scientific terms
- formal/informal style
- tense (present, past, future)
- tone (serious, ironic, persuasive, humorous etc.)
- restricted semantic field (a technical, linguistic term for the writer choosing to use words of a particular type, e.g. all to do with violence, war, nature)

Explain how the writer uses this linguistic device and say whether you think it works or not.

azuzi/Fotolia

Student response to Task A

The advert uses a colourful picture of a young child, a colourful, friendly font, bold writing and a headline.

Examiner's comment

Task A is a Foundation Tier question which is only testing lower-level reading skills. The answer, therefore, simply needs to identify the presentational devices. This student would achieve an F/G grade because of the nature of the question.

How to improve

Be aware of what each question is asking you to do and answer it clearly. Simply identifying a device will always just give you an F/G grade, but this question does not ask for more.

Student response to Task B

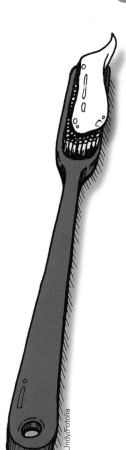

There are several presentational devices used in this advertisement, so I will choose the three most noticeable ones and explain how I think they work. In my opinion, the picture of the child's face with the toothy smile is the most obvious presentational device. The picture reinforces the main message from the manufacturers of the toothpaste, which is that it makes your child's teeth white. The reader's eyes are drawn by the child's smile and we are almost forced to read the copy and skim the rest of the devices used by the advertisers.

Second, the font is sans serif, which advertisers often use to make their copy less formal and more inviting to the reader.

Finally, bright blues are used in the advertisement, portraying a sense of hygiene and cleanliness, as well as brightness and freshness. So, overall, I believe that the presentational devices add to the meaning of the advertisement, which is what they should do.

Examiner's comment

This is a high-level answer because it 'says a lot about a little'. The student fulfils all of the criteria for an A/A* answer and addresses the question in some detail. The candidate uses technical vocabulary (like 'copy' and 'font'), which allows explanation of the advertiser's devices. Just knowing the terminology would earn the candidate few marks: using the terms to explain how the advertisers use the devices helps the student in her conceptualisation, or higher-level idea formation. Note how the student uses the structuring words 'second' and 'finally' to help the examiner through the answer.

How to improve

Use a few more technical terms: for example, use the word 'connotation', instead of simply writing about the colour of the baby's eyes. This term could lead to an even wider explanation of the devices used.

Undy/Fotolia

Student response to Task C

The main organisational device used by the writers of this advertisement is the paragraph, or block, of writing. It is written in dark blue against a light blue background so that it stands out. It is placed next to the photograph of the cute child so that your eyes are naturally drawn to it. The paragraph is not long and includes some highlighted writing so we do not miss the main message. The whole advert is organised like a newspaper, with a headline, a picture and some copy.

Examiner's comment

This is not as good as the answer to Task B, but it would gain a B/C grade. The candidate clearly attempts to answer the question and explains the use of the main organisational device on the page (the paragraph).

How to improve

Go into more detail, or explain more about the overall layout of the page. This was a good point that was undeveloped.

Student response to Task D

The language in this advertisement is overtly persuasive and sounds like the transcript of a television advertisement, with its short sentences, highlighted words and catchphrases. The main linguistic device used by the advertisers, apart from the scientific-sounding additive, is the way they try to make parents feel guilty. 'Don't let your child's smile let you down' sends a subtle, almost coded, message to parents that they could be guilty of neglecting their children's teeth if they don't use this product. Naming the product 'Pegs' is another subtle way of engaging parents' interest, as this is a commonly used term for children's teeth.

Examiner's comment

This is a reasonably detailed response to the question, but does not go into enough detail on any of the valid points made. However, the student clearly shows that he is able to shape and absorb the material to answer the question. In addition, there is evidence of some technical linguistic vocabulary (transcript, catchphrases, coded), which the student uses successfully. This answer would gain a B/C grade.

How to improve

Use technical terms where the meaning is clearly understood and go into as much detail as time will allow.

How can you improve your answers?

There are many opportunities for you to become familiar with the kind of material that you will be asked to read in the English and English Language exams. The more you know about such material *before* you go into the examination, the better you are likely to perform on the day. These opportunities include:

- reading a variety of media wherever you may find them
- evaluating how a range of leaflets on the same subject are presented, e.g. health issues, local transport

- evaluating a range of newspaper front pages, advertisements, fliers, television adverts, logos, cartoons, film openings, CD covers, soap operas etc.
- looking at a range of past papers and focusing on the presentation questions

Now read the front cover of *Chat* magazine which you will eventually have to compare with the front cover of a different magazine.

Task E

Evaluate how well the information is presented on the front page of *Chat* magazine.

Student response to Task E

Here are three attempts at this task, each followed by examiner's comments.

Student answer 1

There are three main parts to this front page of *Chat*. The first thing you notice is the title or name which tells you what the magazine is called. It is quite big and white so it is effective. By the side of it is a large picture of a woman which is also big and effective. The photograph is very colourful and is effective because of the colours. The other main part of this front cover are the bits on the left of the page and at the bottom which tell you about the other stories that will appear in this edition of the magazine. There is a mixture of pictures and words, but it is very colourful and it attracts your attention.

Examiner's comment

The candidate identifies features on the front page and makes simple supported comments, which would earn an E/F grade. This is a good example of an answer that shows the same skill more than once without improving the overall grade, e.g. simply stating that something is effective without explaining why.

How to improve

Identifying is a low-order reading skill, as is 'telling the story' of a text, or paraphrasing. To gain a higher grade you need to **evaluate**.

Student answer 2

I am going to look at how well the front cover of this edition of *Chat* is presented and I am going to evaluate how well done it is. First, it is a particularly 'busy' front page and they have chosen to not have one headline, but have one about a 'Miracle' baby and one about a 'Hubby' faking his own death. They are both in a similar font, but one is blue against white and the other is white against red. I would say that this is not a very successful presentational device because they are too similar. The bottom section of the page advertises four equally lurid stories which seem equally successful in gaining the reader's interest because they are so colourful and include photographs. The photographs of the four stories would appeal to the target audience for this magazine. Finally, there are two more photographs on the left-hand side which relate to the two stories mentioned earlier. There are two more colourful photographs at the top which certainly gain the reader's attention and make the reader want to find out more about these particular stories, especially the 2st cyst!

Examiner's comment

This is a perfect illustration of a performance at a particular grade, this time a Grade C. The student clearly attempts to evaluate some aspects of how well the front page of the magazine is presented. He makes a point (P), finds a relevant example (E) and gives an explanation (E). This shows that the material has been selected and arranged to fit the answer.

How to improve

Do not waste time and effort writing a long introduction that simply restates the question. The first sentence of this answer is pointless because it just repeats the words of the task.

Student answer 3

In my opinion, this front page of a middle-of-the-road magazine is a mess. It is very bitty and it almost puts the reader off with its dog's dinner of presentational devices that do not really complement each other.

First, the most successful aspect of the front page is the use of images, which clearly attract the reader's attention by their appeal to the target audience. There is not simply any image of a woman: the main image is one that most of the readers of this magazine would aspire to. This is a successful presentational device on a few different levels.

Second, the straplines at the bottom of the page offer readers a mixture of emotions and story-lines. The four images all contain faces (or an X-rayed hand!) in an obvious attempt to appeal to the female target audience. But who would offer such stories for publication? These stories are linked to other stories on the front page by the garishly coloured backgrounds which are contrasted with the baby blue next to the baby. Once more, the use of these 'girlie' colours is almost condescending. Finally, we come to the puff at the top right-hand side of the page. It is garishly coloured in the ubiquitous red and yellow seen elsewhere. Both the presentation and the implicit horror of this story about a 2st cyst, with an accompanying picture, would attract prospective readers to buy the magazine.

I think the presentation of this page is very poor. It fulfils its role of trying to sell more copies of the magazine, but it fails to present a front page which successfully advertises what is on offer inside its pages.

Examiner's comment

This answer would gain an A grade, not because it is longer but because it shows that the student has absorbed the material and shaped it to fit the question. Notice that, like the F-grade candidate, this student spotted the main image, but instead of simply describing it she has commented on how the magazine uses it. The skills required to earn a Grade A include:

* clear and detailed understanding of what the question is asking
* careful and logical argument, backed up with examples
* material fully absorbed and shaped for purpose
* sophisticated and convincing use of technical terminology to describe media concepts

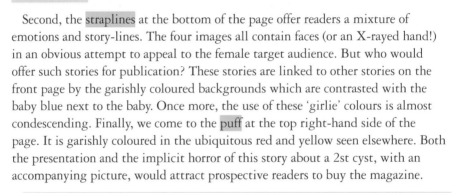

How to improve

Use technical terminology convincingly and in a way that is helpful, as a sort of shorthand. For example, the words 'strapline' and 'puff' used in this answer are recognised terms in journalism.

Assessment for learning

What skills do you think are demonstrated by each of the highlighted examples in the final answer? Discuss them with a partner and explain how they exemplify the Grade A descriptors above.

Remember: all candidates should be able to spot material; the better ones are able to evaluate it.

Combining **AO2(i)** and **AO2(iii)**

You may be asked to compare, or make cross-references between, the use of presentational devices in the English or English Language examination.

How is this assessed

This is usually assessed if you are required to read two or more items on the same subject, or if they use devices in similar or different ways.

We have already compared two texts for understanding, AO2(i) on pages 8–9, but we are now going to start to put the Assessment Objectives together and compare the uses of linguistic/grammatical, structural and presentational features, AO2(iii).

Grade A	A complete answer which compares all parts of the question equally well.
Grade C	A clear and structured attempt to compare.
Grade F	An unstructured attempt to compare, but tends to identify features.

Parts of these three basic grade descriptors should now be beginning to sound familiar.

How can you improve your answers?

To gain a grade higher than a D you have to make a clear comparison, finding either a similarity, a difference, or both. To make your comparisons clear you should continue to use words and phrases such as those in the table on page 8.

Remember: you can also use comparatives such as **bigger, louder, brighter, more colourful** and **clearer**. It is a good idea to compare things which are similar or different in obvious ways too.

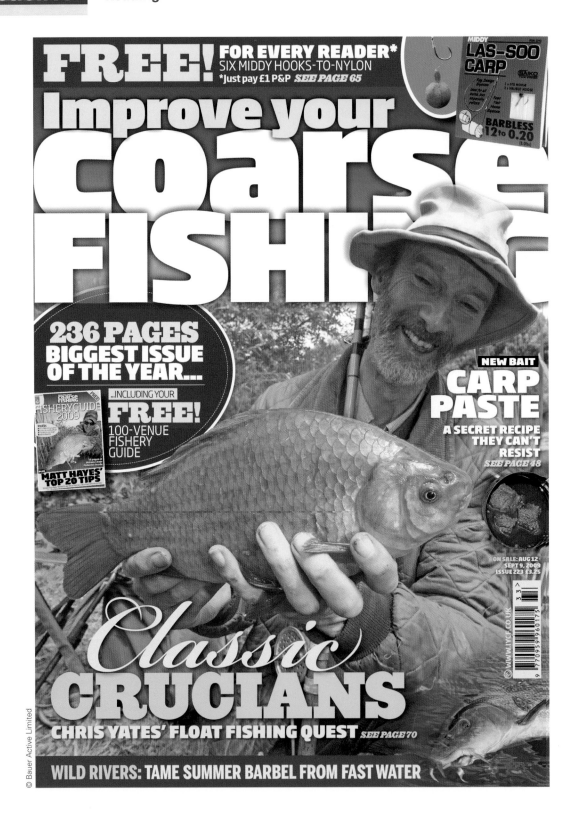

Task A

Read the front page of *Coarse Fishing*.

1 Identify the typical magazine features on the front page of *Coarse Fishing*, using appropriate technical terms.

2 Compare the ways in which these two magazine front pages are presented by copying and completing the following tables.

	Chat	*Coarse Fishing*
Similarities	They both advertise what is inside the magazine	
	They are similarly laid out	
	Etc.	

	Chat	*Coarse Fishing*
Differences	Not much text to read	Has more detail
	Pink and baby blue	Manly camouflage
	Lots of small pictures	One main image
	Etc.	Etc.

3 Use the tables that you have prepared to answer the following question.

Compare how:

- presentational
- organisational
- linguistic

devices are used try to persuade someone to buy these two different magazines and comment on their purposes.

When you come to write comparisons in the examination you should use the **point, example, explain** structure, so part of your answer to Task A Question 3 might read:

Point: '*Both* front pages use devices to persuade people to buy their magazines and they share many devices. *However*, they differ in how well these devices are used,

Example: for example they both use images,

Explain: but *Chat* uses too many and makes the front page over-fussy, thereby detracting from the overall visual appeal.'

Student response to Task A Q3

Student answer 1

The presentation of these two front covers is surprisingly similar. They both have large titles, a main picture of a person in a similar position on the page and details of other features within the magazine, but the *Coarse Fishing* has far fewer words to read on the front page and far fewer pictures.

The pages are laid out in the same way with very little difference between them, including the placing of the main photographs in similar places. On the other hand, *Chat* tends to look a bit fussy and cluttered because there are so many stories mentioned on the front page with so many extra pictures.

There is very little language on the front page of *Coarse Fishing*, but there is more on the front of *Chat*.

The main purpose of both front pages is to sell the magazine by interesting a prospective reader in the features which are included inside.

Student answer 2

The surprising and almost eerie thing about these two front pages is how strikingly similar they are. Considering that *Coarse Fishing* is a single interest magazine with a specific audience in mind, it has taken on a lot of the characteristics of mainstream, more populist magazines like *Chat*. From a distance, the two magazine front covers look disconcertingly alike with their mastheads, straplines, headlines, photographs and use of colour. However, on closer study, *Coarse Fishing* uses a little less colour on its front page and includes far fewer images. Additionally, *Coarse Fishing* is presented in a more coherent way with an overall theme to the presentation: *Chat* is presented in a more haphazard, or 'chatty', way with its more amateurish photographs and sensational colours which link with the sensational stories. *Coarse Fishing* is more subtle in its use of muted camouflage tones and its more conservative list of features.

As mentioned in the previous paragraph, the two magazine front covers are broadly similar in presentation and layout, but there are subtle differences. *Chat* has a huge number of photo stories advertised on the page and they tend to dwarf and over-power the rest of the layout. It is understandable why this has been done because this magazine is in competition with many other such magazines and it has to make an instant and sensationalised appeal and proposes to 'chat' with the reader. The layout of *Coarse Fishing* is similarly dominated by one feature; the perfectly appropriate image of a fisherman holding a fish in this case. There is, however, a better balance in the layout between title, straplines and picture. The whole front page seems to be more consistent and it all fits in with coarse fish, fishing and men. *Chat* is much more of a dog's breakfast of clashing colours and trashy stories.

The language one the front pages is also quite different. *Chat* tends to use sensational adjectives and nouns in its copy, like 'killer slime', 'Weetabix babe', 'jealous ex', 'YUCK!' and 'GULP!' This use of language attempts to influence the reader's response and to sensationalise an already sensational space. There is also a lot of first person used on this front page to show how personalised and intimate some of these stories are. On occasions, the language and presentation are linked together, like in the sub-headline, *'and broke our kids' hearts…'* in order to make double impact.

On the other hand, *Coarse Fishing* is more measured in its choice of language, but even its writers use a lot of adjectives for effect, e.g. 'Classic Crucians' and 'wild rivers'. There is an element of journalese in this choice of lexis, but it is more the sort of language expected of a quality single interest magazine. After all, it does include a carp paste with a secret recipe that no carp will be able to resist, with a picture!

Finally, the two magazines have similar purposes in that they both want to attract floating buyers (excuse the pun!) to pick up their periodical from the newsstand, but *Coarse Fishing* is less blousy and blatant in its approach. *Chat* almost exists on passing trade, so it has to advertise its wares in a colourful and eye-catching manner.

Student answer 3

Chat has a big photograph, some smaller pictures and a lot of human interest stories on the front. There is quite a lot of writing and there are quite a lot of different colours. *Coarse Fishing* has got a lot less writing on the front and it has a big photograph of a fisherman who has caught a fish. The writing in *Chat* is easy to understand and there are an awful lot of different types of stories. *Coarse Fishing* has some difficult words like 'Classic Crucians', but it is quite easy to understand.

Chat is laid out like the front page of a newspaper and *Coarse Fishing* looks more like a typical glossy magazine. I think *Chat* is laid out better.

The purpose of *Chat* is to tell people about the terrible things that have happened to other people, to make the reader feel not so bad. The purpose of *Coarse Fishing* is very much contained in the title: it wants to help you become a better coarse fisherman.

Assessment for Learning

1 With a partner, re-read the grade descriptors on page 23 and copy them out if necessary.

2 Place these three student answers in rank order.

3 Justify your rank order, by referring to details from each answer to back up your decisions.

4 Identify:
   • one thing that each student has done well and describe what it is that they have done well
   • one thing that each student could have done better

5 Share your thoughts with the rest of your class.

AO2(iv)

Understand texts in their social, cultural and historical contexts

Where is AO2(iv) assessed?

This has never been a specific Assessment Objective on its own before. Previously, this was part of another AO and it was largely ignored. However, now that it is one of the four reading AOs, we are going to give it due attention. It is mainly assessed under controlled conditions where it assumes great importance.

How is AO2(iv) assessed?

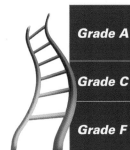

Grade A	A complete answer with the material being shaped and absorbed for purpose with a convincing use of technical terminology and each of the three aspects being addressed.
Grade C	A clear and structured response to the question which selects and comments on different aspects of social, cultural and historical contexts.
Grade F	An unstructured attempt to engage with the task, with the student tending to paraphrase and to identify generalised examples of how texts are contextualised.

How can you improve your answers?

There are a number of different ways of getting better at this particular skill. Here are some suggestions:

- carry over skills from pre-1914 prose and pre-1914 poetry into media and non-fiction texts
- carry over skills from media studies
- use source material in your history course as comparative texts with modern non-fiction and media

Task A

Compare how the:

- layout
- language
- purpose
- audience

Remember: when a question is split into bullet points, you should try to spend an equal amount of time on each bullet.

of the two advertisements for skin care show that they were written at very different times.

Student response to Task A

Student answer 1

The 'Nivea' advert shows a young woman's face which is perfect and has no pimples or spots. Probably, they have air-brushed out any skin problems so that she looks perfect. This is aimed at women and there is not much language at all. The 'Pomeroy Skin Food' advert has a lot more language and it does not even show a woman's face. It suggests that you will look like a lady in a boudoir if you use this skin product.

Examiner's comment

This is a perfect example of an 'unstructured response' that simply 'paraphrases', or tells the story of the adverts. The student does not compare, but just juxtaposes responses to the two items. This answer would gain a Grade E/F.

How to improve

Draw up a simple table/plan to ensure that you actually answer the question in front of you.

Student answer 2

The layout of the two advertisements is very different. The Nivea advert is mainly taken up with a full-face picture of a young woman with perfect skin and with a pot of the cream centrally placed and a headline at the top of the page. On the other hand, the Pomeroy advert is dominated by a drawing of a woman in a boudoir, with about the same amount of writing, but in a much smaller space. This makes the layout of this advert look cluttered.

Similarly, the language used in both adverts is very different. The language used in the Nivea advert is very definite as it tells the reader that it is 'the best' and that 'wrinkles hate it'. This style of telling the reader what to think is repeated throughout the advert. The Pomeroy advert uses more formal language which is because it was written in the past.

The purpose of both adverts is to sell their product and to make rather inflated claims for the product they are selling. They also both try to suggest that if you use their product then you will look like the person in the advert.

Again, the audiences of both adverts are similar in that they are both aimed at women who believe that they have a problem with wrinkles and other skin problems. However, the Pomeroy product is aimed at 'posher' women than the Nivea cream because the woman in the picture is in a boudoir and is dressed like a lady. Also, the language is posher in the Pomeroy advert because it uses words like 'eradicates' and it also uses alliteration in the headline.

Examiner's comment

This is a clear C-grade response because the student addresses each of the bullet points in a structured way and actually answers the question, which is to compare how the two adverts show that they were written at different times. The comparison words and phrases have been highlighted to make it obvious that the student is addressing the main objective of this question.

The student is, however, rather mechanical in responding to each bullet and almost identifies each difference or similarity without really commenting on it. This is a good example of how a student can gain marks by attempting the question as set and by applying a structure to the response. In this case, that structure is a paragraph about each of the bullets and a comparison within each paragraph.

How to improve

Develop the skill of integrating comparisons and trying to come up with less obvious comparisons, like in the next student's response.

Student answer 3

It is very obvious that these two adverts were written at different times even from a cursory glance, but it is interesting to examine the ways in which they are similar and different. The most obvious difference between the two is the size and the ways in which the images of women have been integrated into the layouts. The Nivea advert is 'in your face' in that it is dominated by an image of the woman's perfect skin. This layout technique allows the advertisers to make the page resemble a mirror in which the reader can compare her own image. This comparison is bound to be detrimental. The much smaller Pomeroy advert is also dominated by the female form, but this time, the reader is given a lifestyle image which suggests that if the reader uses Pomeroy products, she will end up being like this lady in a boudoir. The layout definitely suggests a different period in history, because the layout coyly shows a lady's back and only suggests a hint of skin by showing her neck and forearms. This coyness points to a difference in attitude and social perspective.

It is, however, in the language that there are the greatest differences. The Nivea advert is peremptory in its style in that it *tells* the reader, by using a definite form of the verb (e.g. 'hate', 'reduces', 'Proven'). It also uses dubious scientific-sounding language to back up its claims that it gets rid of wrinkles. By using scientific-sounding terms, like 'Q10' and 'unique Energy Complex', it persuades the reader that the whole product has a scientific basis. By personifying the product ('wrinkles hate it'), the advertiser conveys power onto the product by making it something that wrinkles actively hate. On the other hand, the Pomeroy product is driven more by narrative in its approach. The style is more personal as it addresses the reader directly; even though it is in the third person, it is quite personal. There is also an interesting use of alliteration in the heading which stresses the fact that the reader will share the lifestyle of the lady whose back is showing.

Both adverts have the same overall purpose, which is to sell their product to women and to help them with their skin-care problems. The direct gaze of the Nivea woman suggests an openness and directness, which is reflected by the almost magic qualities of the cream because it shines and glistens in the pot. With its scientific language and perfect appearance, it suggests a miracle cure from wrinkles. The Pomeroy cream also suggests a sort of miracle in that it tries to tie the reader in by suggesting that they will never be able to live without it after having used it ('it is impossible to imagine'). Its purpose is also linked with language, audience and layout, because the advertiser is attempting to connect all aspects of the advert's appeal.

Finally, the audiences are obviously similar because they are both unashamedly aimed at women and prey on a woman's fear of ageing and getting wrinkles. They are both aimed at the same age range, but they are subtly aimed at different social classes. The Nivea advert is more universal in its appeal to all classes. However, the Pomeroy product, even by dint of its name, is aiming at a more affluent audience. The layout and language all suggest an upper-middle-class audience, especially the address and name of the person to whom all correspondence should be sent.

Examiner's comment

This is a complete answer which comments on different aspects of each bullet and goes into some detail. 'Saying a lot about a little' is often a descriptor for A/A* grade performance.

The other strength of this answer, which lifts it into this grade, is the way it links the different elements listed in the bullet points. This is the ability 'to absorb and shape'. In practice, it means that the student can read a whole item, absorb it, keep it in his/her mind's eye, compare different aspects of the first item with a second one, then shape the response to fit the actual demands of the question. This student shows how the apparently separate bullet points are all, in fact, linked, and is beginning to make 'big picture links' between meaning, layout, presentation etc. These links are equally important when reading non-fiction, media, poetry, prose or drama.

How to improve

Develop this skill by using it whenever and wherever you are asked to carry out a reading assessment.

B

Writing

Chapter 2

Assessment Objectives for writing (1)

Writing makes up 40% of the marks for GCSE English. Writing is an important skill because being able to write well for different purposes helps us in many situations in our daily lives.

The many different types of writing can be split into two broad categories: non-fiction texts and creative texts. To put it simply, non-fiction texts are factual or concerned with factual information, whereas creative texts are fictional.

Successful writers understand what they are being asked to write about and create texts that fit the audience and purpose for which they are writing. It's really important to make the right choices in your writing tasks so that you can show off your skills to the examiner to the best of your ability. In the examination and controlled assessment tasks, you need to read the questions carefully and interpret what they are asking you to do before beginning your answers. One good way of doing this is to underline the key words in each question so you are clear about what you are being asked to write.

The activities and advice in this section will help you to develop the skills that are essential to good writing. Make sure your writing has the 'X-Factor!'

AO3

For GCSE English, your writing will be assessed against the following Assessment Objectives (AOs). The key words are emboldened. These will be explained below.

AO3(i)	• **Communicate clearly** and **imaginatively**, **using**, **adapting** and **selecting vocabulary** appropriate to task and purpose in ways that engage the reader.
AO3(ii)	• **Organise** information and ideas into **structured** and **sequenced** sentences, paragraphs and whole texts, using a variety of **linguistic structural features** to support **cohesion** and overall **coherence**.
AO3(iii)	• Use a range of **sentence structures** for **clarity, purpose** and **effect** with **accurate punctuation** and **spelling**.

This Assessment Objective, AO3, is known as AO4 in the English Language specifications. The content is exactly the same and for ease of reference and to avoid confusion, it is mainly referred to as AO3 in this book.

Where is AO3 assessed?

This AO is assessed just about everywhere you are being assessed for writing: it is the fundamental test of whether you can write well and in an appropriate style for the intended audience and purpose.

In the GCSE English and English Language courses you will gain your writing marks in Unit 1 and Unit 3. In the English course, the writing section of each of these units is worth 20%, making up 40% of your total marks. In the English Language course, the writing section of Unit 1 is worth 20%, but the writing part of Unit 3 is only worth 15%, making up 35% of your total marks.

In Unit 1, Section B, you will need to show that you can produce non-fiction texts to a good standard that matches your GCSE grade expectations. This will be assessed in a 1-hour examination, through two compulsory writing tasks, a shorter writing task and a longer writing task. Unit 1 is covered in more detail in Chapter 3.

In Unit 3, you will be assessed for your skills in producing creative texts. This will be in the form of a 'controlled assessment', for which you will be given a total time allocation of 3–4 hours. This will be assessed in supervised conditions. The difference between this specification and the old one is that you will not be allowed to take this piece of work home to finish and in your final assessment your teacher cannot give you feedback. In English the creative writing task is worth a total of 40 marks. In English Language the task is out of a total of 30 marks.

How is AO3 assessed?

Writing tasks will usually be based on a variety of non-fiction genres. Some of the tasks will contain a functional skills element, for example giving someone information; the other tasks will ask you to write for specific audiences and purposes, adapting your 'writing style' so that it is fit for purpose and works like a real text.

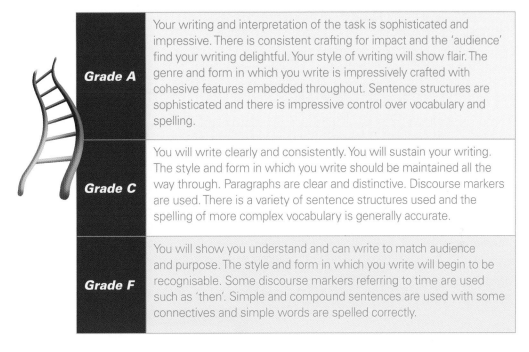

Grade A	Your writing and interpretation of the task is sophisticated and impressive. There is consistent crafting for impact and the 'audience' find your writing delightful. Your style of writing will show flair. The genre and form in which you write is impressively crafted with cohesive features embedded throughout. Sentence structures are sophisticated and there is impressive control over vocabulary and spelling.
Grade C	You will write clearly and consistently. You will sustain your writing. The style and form in which you write should be maintained all the way through. Paragraphs are clear and distinctive. Discourse markers are used. There is a variety of sentence structures used and the spelling of more complex vocabulary is generally accurate.
Grade F	You will show you understand and can write to match audience and purpose. The style and form in which you write will begin to be recognisable. Some discourse markers referring to time are used such as 'then'. Simple and compound sentences are used with some connectives and simple words are spelled correctly.

In order to gain a Grade C or above against this Assessment Objective you need to think about what it means in practice:

- You must understand different writing formats.
- You must be able to develop texts that match style, audience, purpose and form.
- You must be able to use a range of sentence structures.
- You need to be able to use a range of punctuation correctly.

> **Remember:** when you are writing, you must write according to **style**, **audience** and **purpose** (SAP).

Unit 3: producing creative texts

It is important to select a question or task for assessment that will give you the opportunity to show off your skills, not necessarily the one that you would like to write about because you 'like' the topic. For example, a question on writing to describe gives you a real chance to craft your writing and use all the literary devices you have been taught.

You must also be equipped with the right language to answer the questions. Before you begin the assessment, remind yourself with a few quick notes of the features of each kind of writing. Practise planning and beginning different types of questions, bearing in mind what the examiner is looking for.

Task A

Describe someone you know well personally who has made an impression on you. **Explain** why he/she is important to you.

Consider how you are going to approach this question:

- Note the key words in bold.
- Consider who you are going to write about carefully.
- Think about how this person has made an impact on you.
- Think about why this person is important to you.

Copy and complete the following table to help plan your answer.

Consider the question	Add the details...
Who is this person?	
How has this person made an impact on you?	
Why is this person important to you?	

Remember: there are two parts to this question, **describing** and **explaining**. Refer to both in your plan.

AO3(i)

Communicate clearly and imaginatively, using, adapting and selecting vocabulary appropriate to task and purpose in ways that engage the reader

Key words	What the key words mean
communicate clearly	You express your ideas clearly so the reader knows what it is you are writing about.
imaginatively	You use your imagination to interpret the question.
adapting and selecting vocabulary	You use vocabulary which matches what you have been asked to write about and you use ways and techniques which make the reader interested in your work.

We will now look at two contrasting student responses to Task A above.

Student responses to Task A

Student answer 1

The gaunt, shabby attire that I had once found repulsive, was something I had now grown accustomed to. The pungent odour that lingered permanently on this unkempt, dishevelled soul made me wince, only occasionally, with disgust.

Arron was now no more financially stable than he was then, but nonetheless, this parasite of society and I were now firm friends.

Looking back three long, interminable years to when we first met, outside on the damp, soggy pavement, he sat there, almost planted, like a badly-constructed snowman, with a tattered, brown coat that was his only shelter from the bitterly cold night. My first real encounter with this rootless, friendless, homeless man was to change my life forever...

Examiner's comment

The main ideas are expressed clearly. The reader immediately understands that this person has made a lasting impression. The candidate's choice of subject, the homeless man, is imaginative and creates interest and engagement. This answer fulfils all the requirements for an A grade for this AO.

Assessment for Learning

Identify three things which this student has done well and identify two things that could have been better. Discuss your findings with a partner.

Student answer 2

The person who made a real impression on me was my best friend, in the street where I lived. I really liked Sabeen because she always helped me when things went wrong. She is like a strong wall to lean on when I have problems at home or at school. Sabeen has long, dark brown hair and a distinctive smile that I can recognise from a distance.

Sometimes, Sabeen has had a problem and I have been able to help her too. She has been having a really difficult time because her parents have been thinking about moving to Canada but she still has time to help me with the things I find difficult. A few days ago, I had to tell her my really sad news...

Examiner's comment

The main ideas match the style and purpose of the question. There is clear depth and detail in this response. Vocabulary and stylistic devices are used to create effects. This answer would achieve a C grade.

Assessment for Learning

1 Identify two things which this student has done well and identify one thing that could have been better. Discuss your findings with a partner.
2 Discuss the differences between the A-grade and C-grade answers with a partner and try to agree on at least two of them, giving reasons.

AO3(ii)

Organise information and ideas into structured and sequenced sentences, paragraphs and whole texts, using a variety of linguistic structural features to support cohesion and overall coherence

Key words	What the key words mean
organise information and ideas	You can arrange your work in an organised way with a clear structure.
structured and sequenced sentences	Your sentences are well constructed and link well together.
linguistic structural features	This is the way you use language in a text and how you put it together.
cohesion and overall coherence	You create well-thought-out links between successive paragraphs and successive sentences.

Organisational devices

The examiner will be looking for the following devices to indicate that you have organised and structured your work:

not necessarily a narrative

well-structured ideas

awareness of form, style, audience and purpose

well-linked paragraphs

a clear focus on the topic: engaging

a range of punctuation

crafted language, extensive vocabulary, power verbs, figurative language, e.g. literary devices such as similes, metaphors, alliterations, juxtoposition and oxymorons

a thoughtful and imaginative viewpoint

a variety of sentence types/lengths

use of senses

For two of the key devices above, an example of their usage is given below.

Example 1

Opening paragraph demonstrating a thoughtful and imaginative viewpoint:

Walking along the dusty embankment in the relentless summer heat, the sun beat down on the distant figure. I watched mesmerised for a while…

Task A

Continue the paragraph in Example 1, using thoughtful, imaginative images and vocabulary.

Example 2

Opening paragraph demonstrating use of senses:

The pungent odour invaded the air like an unwelcome stranger. I almost lunged backwards with the shock, grazing my tightly clutched knuckles on the rough wooden gate…

Task B

Continue the description in Example 2 using at least two of the senses in the next four sentences you write. Remember it all has to fit together well.

Possible beginnings/interpretations

Whenever you are asked to write imaginatively, try to be creative with how you begin your piece.

Task C

Look back at the examples you did for Tasks A and B above and write alternative openings.

Task D

Describe the place where you would most like to live.

Remember: make sure you include the organisational devices listed opposite to show that you have understood how to use these techniques.

Assessment for Learning

Look back at the criteria for Grade A or C (depending on your target grade) in producing creative texts on page 35 and highlight and label where you have fulfilled each part of the criteria in your work. Write a brief examiner's comment. A short example has been done for you below:

Student response to Task D

The fragrant smell of fresh air filled the whole beach like a welcome visitor. The group of strangers in the distance seemed far away yet friendly. Yesterday and the unhappiness it had brought did not seem to matter now. I was lost. Warm, white sand trickled over my skin and the fearsome sun beat down on my delicate face. A slumbering paradise was enveloped by sapphire waters.

Where else would I live now? Here was everything I had ever wanted; the family I had come to care about; the friends I had come to love…

Corel

Examiner's comment

The response shows clarity of thought and communicates successfully. Informative and descriptive ideas engage the reader, for example, effective use of alliteration and metaphors encompassing personification. Well-thought-out ideas are presented. Sentences vary in structure and are accurately presented. Standard English is used appropriately. The way the candidate writes is consistent. This piece of writing fulfils the criteria for grade B.

AO3(iii)

Use a range of sentence structures for clarity, purpose and effect with accurate punctuation and spelling

Key words	What the key words mean
sentence structures	This means how you put sentences together and construct them.
clarity	Your writing is clear.
purpose	This is the reason for which your text is written.
effect	This is the impression you create with what you write.
accurate punctuation	You use punctuation in the correct places.
spelling	Your spelling is accurate.

Where is AO3(iii) assessed?

This part of AO3 is assessed just about everywhere you are being assessed for writing and it is important that you grasp the technicalities of what makes good writing.

How is AO3(iii) assessed?

There are up to 15 marks available for this part of AO3. It is especially important in differentiating between C-grade answers and the higher grades of B, A and A*. Writers at the higher levels of performance do not simply write down the first phrase or sentence that comes into their heads, they go beyond that first thought and consciously craft their writing.

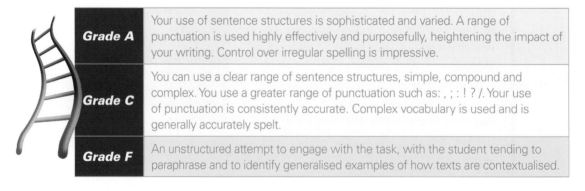

Grade A	Your use of sentence structures is sophisticated and varied. A range of punctuation is used highly effectively and purposefully, heightening the impact of your writing. Control over irregular spelling is impressive.
Grade C	You can use a clear range of sentence structures, simple, compound and complex. You use a greater range of punctuation such as: , ; : ! ? / . Your use of punctuation is consistently accurate. Complex vocabulary is used and is generally accurately spelt.
Grade F	An unstructured attempt to engage with the task, with the student tending to paraphrase and to identify generalised examples of how texts are contextualised.

Sentence structure

We need to consider the most important aspect of this part of this AO: sentence structure or the way we 'string our words together'. We will look at punctuation and the use of conjunctions in more detail in Chapter 3.

What do we need to create sentences? Well, I think you will agree that a car mechanic needs the right toolkit to do the job properly. Learning about different types of sentences and how to create and use them will give you the right toolkit to help you find success in communicating clearly and effectively with your audience.

Types of sentences

There are three key types of sentences:

simple sentences   **compound sentences**   **complex sentences**

Simple sentences

These are sentences that contain only *one* independent main clause. This means that they can stand alone and make sense. For example, the following are all simple sentences:

'Help!'   **'Alice.'**

Tony leaves.   **Sana left home.**

However, they could mean different things when used in different contexts.

For example, in the first sentence, 'help' is a **verb** which suggests urgency and need of assistance. In the second sentence, 'Alice' is a **noun,** which could suggest a number of things: Alice is wanted or needed, Alice is to blame, Alice has been found out etc. In order to clarify what a sentence means we can combine a verb and a noun to add more specific meaning as in the third sentence, 'Tony leaves'.

In the last sentence an **object** (home) has been added give it a more exact meaning.' Home', though still a noun, is known as an object because this is the thing or place that Sana has left.

Task A

Now, following the pattern in the examples above, try to make simple sentences of your own.

1 .... (Use a **verb**.)
2 .... (Use a **noun**.)
3 .... (Combine a **verb** and a **noun**.)
4 .... (Use a **verb**, a **noun** and an **object**.)

Tip: punctuation helps make meaning clear. Make sure you keep this in mind.

> **Remember:** simple sentences have a simple structure and one main clause.

Compound sentences

The word '**compound**' means made up of two or more parts. Compound sentences are made up of *two* or more simple sentences and contain *two* independent main clauses, which are usually joined together by a **conjunction** (a word that connects, such as 'and', 'but', 'then' or 'so'). The independent clauses are of *equal* value in the sentence. Using a slightly longer sentence can add more of a flow to your writing and stop it from being too abrupt. For example:

> Hari watched television **then** went outside.

(Can you spot the two independent main clauses? They are separated by the conjunction '**then**'.)

Task B

Try completing the following sentences to create compound sentences of your own.

1 Jan laughed .... ran away. *(Add a **conjunction**.)*

2 Robert forgot his homework but .... an excuse. *(Add a **verb**.)*

3 The old man coughed .... in the cold. *(Add a **conjunction**, followed by a **verb**.)*

Sometimes, it is more appropriate to use a **semi-colon (;)** to separate the two main clauses instead of a conjunction. This helps to avoid a string of sentences that are all joined by conjunctions and sound a little monotonous; especially in more serious types of writing. For example:

> The dark figure was close; he could feel its breath.
> The night was dark; the stars were like lights.

In these examples the two parts or main clauses are connected to the same topic. You can also use a semi-colon to link clauses on different subjects when using a conjunction does not help to make the meaning of the sentence clear. For example:

> Daniyal was still new to the town; Sabrina had lived in her village for two years.

Task C

Create two examples of compound sentences in which the two main clauses are separated by a semi-colon.

> **Remember:** compound sentences have two independent main clauses.

Complex sentences

These are sentences that are a little more complicated. They contain at least **one independent clause** and **one dependent clause**. The dependent clause is also known as the **subordinate clause**. The dependent clause cannot stand alone; it relies or depends on the independent main clause in order for it to make sense.

Dependent clauses are always introduced by conjunctions such as 'because', 'if', 'when', 'until', 'although', 'if', 'so that', 'unless' etc. For example:

> He will freeze at night *unless he can find a warm blanket.*
> *When* Aaron proposed, *Sara was more shocked than anything else.*
> He gave up a good job *so that he could spend more time with his family.*

Task D

Using the examples above to guide you, complete the sentences below by adding a *new* dependent clause to each.

1 He will freeze at night **unless** ....

2 **When** Aaron proposed, ...

3 He gave up a good job **so that** ....

You may even wish to be more adventurous and create three complex sentences of your own from scratch.

> **Remember:** complex sentences have a more complicated structure, and have at least one independent main clause and one dependent clause.

Putting the jigsaw together ...

What does using a range of sentence structures for clarity, purpose and effect with accurate punctuation and spelling look like in GCSE writing?

You should now have an idea of the main types of sentences. The next thing you have to consider is how to put them together in a piece of writing so that you meet the Assessment Objective fully. It's a bit like putting together the pieces of a jigsaw. With practice you develop an ability to decide where each piece should go. Before getting it right you may experiment and try out where certain pieces could go. With practice you will develop your ability to decide which types of sentences to use and when to use them. You may even decide to move the position of words or sentences or to change the types of sentences you use. All this is a perfectly acceptable, and expected, part of becoming a successful writer.

Let's use some of these sentence types in a passage to see what kind of effect they can have.

Task E

Describe the ideal place you would escape to if you were given a choice.

Student response to Task E

This is my special place. My only place; where no-one can find me. My mind is the place where I escape to when things get too much for me.

Effervescent and enticing, this is a fable-like chamber. It is a place full of great open spaces so that I can escape from reality. There are rooms called chambers everywhere. I go there at different times: when I am a little sad; when I am lonely; when I am mixed up; even when I have something to celebrate! It's a bit like a 'mini holiday' although sometimes it only lasts for a few seconds. A single second!

I have a precious chamber in my mind which keeps all my thoughts safe when I don't want to share them with anyone. Would you? Although it's not always easy, it's still a great place to be and I would choose it anytime. I love it. It's like a bedroom but with no door. Inconspicuously built on foundations of solitude; my secret garden…

Examiner's comment

A variety of sentence structures are used in this piece of writing, which has an impressive effect on the reader. The way punctuation is used enhances the purpose of the writing and therefore heightens its impact on the reader. Vocabulary choices are sophisticated. Spelling of less commonplace vocabulary such as 'effervescent' is accurate. If you read the Grade A descriptors, this would just about fulfil all of them.

How to improve

Identify some of the sentence types you have read about in this answer. Locate at least one example of each type: simple, compound and complex.

Assessment for Learning

Study your own answer closely. Identify and label where you meet, exceed or fall below the A or C grade criteria (depending on your target grade), found in the table on page 35.

And finally…

You are the mechanic and as such you should be able to engineer your writing. *You* are a painter with a blank canvas who can create things from your imagination. *You* are a make-up artist behind the scenes of a play who can 'dress up' things so that the audience sees things the way you want them. The end product of your writing is what you make it. Sometimes we just have to work at it and practise to get it right — that's what real writers do!

picsfive/Fotolia

B

Writing

Chapter 3

Assessment Objectives for writing (2)

In English and English Language the writing section of Unit 1 makes up 20% of the total marks for your GCSE. Writing, as discussed earlier, is an important skill and in real life we have to be able to write texts which can explain, argue or advise within the contexts of everyday life. You may also know this as a style of writing called 'non-fiction'. Although at this stage of your life, you are usually just preparing to express yourself in such situations within school life, there is sometimes the need in real life to be able to present what you say in a manner that is both acceptable to others and effectively presented to 'be heard.' Therefore, it is your skills in making realistic representations in your written pieces of work or answers that will be assessed in Unit 1.

In Chapters 3–5, we will look at different forms of writing, probable audiences, a selection of purposes for writing and a range of different styles, all in the context of the Assessment Objectives and grade criteria for writing. All these elements are of course interlinked and often determine how each one will become part of the whole text. You need to craft your writing to demonstrate your skills to the examiner and gain the best possible marks that you can.

AO3

For GCSE English, your writing will be assessed against the following Assessment Objectives (AOs) in both Units 1 and 3. The key words are emboldened — these were explained in Chapter 2 (see pages 36, 38 and 40). Note that at least one third of the available marks will be allocated to AO3(iii).

AO3(i)	• **Communicate clearly** and **imaginatively**, **using**, **adapting** and **selecting vocabulary** appropriate to task and purpose in ways that engage the reader.
AO3(ii)	• **Organise** information and ideas into **structured** and **sequenced** sentences, paragraphs and whole texts, using a variety of **linguistic structural features** to support **cohesion** and overall **coherence**.
AO3(iii)	• Use a range of **sentence structures** for **clarity, purpose** and **effect** with **accurate punctuation** and **spelling**.

This Assessment Objective, AO3, is known as AO4 in the English Language specifications. The content is exactly the same and for ease of reference and to avoid confusion, it is mainly referred to as AO3 in this book.

Where is AO3 assessed in Unit 1?

In Unit 1, this AO is assessed in Section B of the examination paper. As is the case in Unit 3, this is a fundamental test of whether you can write well, with clarity and in an appropriate style for the intended purpose and audience. Section B of Unit 1 has a weighting of 40 marks, equivalent to 20% of your total GCSE marks. This unit is common to both GCSE English and GCSE English Language.

How is AO3 assessed in Unit 1?

In both the Higher and Foundation Tiers of the examination papers, you will be asked to complete two compulsory writing tasks for Unit 1: one shorter task which is worth 16 marks and one longer task worth 24 marks, making a total of 40 marks. You will be asked to write in a range of genres for specific purposes, adapting your style so that it is fit for the purpose for which you are writing. All three parts of AO3 will be assessed in each question.

Functional skills elements are embedded in this unit, allowing you to show that you can be a competent and confident writer in situations that could occur in everyday life.

The different writing formats and writing styles and purposes are covered in more detail in Chapters 4 and 5 respectively.

Unit 1: shorter writing task

The shorter writing task in Unit 1 is marked out of 16:

- A maximum of 10 marks will be awarded for **communication** and **organisation**.
- A maximum of 6 marks will be awarded for using a range of **sentence structures** for **clarity, purpose** and **effect** with **accurate punctuation** and **spelling**.

AO3(i) and **AO3(ii)**: communication and organisation

AO3(i): communicate clearly and imaginatively, using, adapting and selecting vocabulary appropriate to task and purpose in ways that engage the reader

AO3(ii): organise information and ideas into structured and sequenced sentences, paragraphs and whole texts, using a variety of linguistic structural features to support cohesion and overall coherence

How are AO3(i) and AO3(ii) assessed?

Grade A	**Communication:** your writing, interpretation and communication of the task is '**convincing** and **compelling**'. Your writing is engaging and ideas are detailed and developed, and sometimes abstract. The tone is appropriate and effective. You evoke a response from the reader. Use of linguistic devices such as rhetorical questions and hyperbole is effective. Discursive markers are extensive and controlled extensively.
	Organisation: you write the whole of the text in continuous prose and paragraphs enhance meaning. Structural features are used appropriately and effectively. Complex ideas are presented coherently
Grade C	**Communication:** your writing, interpretation and communication of the task show '**clarity** and **success**'. Your writing is engaging and ideas are detailed, developed, and descriptive. The tone is appropriate and sometimes subtle. You clearly communicate the intention and purpose of your writing. Use of linguistic devices such as rhetorical questions and hyperbole is appropriate. Discursive markers are effective.
	Organisation: you use paragraphs effectively. You begin to use structural features, such as different paragraph lengths, appropriately. Ideas are well-presented in sentences.
Grade F	**Communication:** your communication of the task is '**limited**'. You communicate a few ideas and engage the reader with some reference to them. The register may vary between formal and slang and neither may be sustained. Rhetorical devices or lists may not always be effective, with limited vocabulary. Informative markers are not often used.
	Organisation: your use of paragraphs is erratic if they are used. You may use one-sentence paragraphs.

Key words success ladder for AO3(i) and AO3(ii)

	Communication (C)	Organisation (O)
Grade A *'convincing and compelling'*	• Communication shows clarity of thought, is convincing and compelling. • Detailed, developed, sometimes abstract, ideas convince the reader. • Purpose, intention, objective is sustained. • Linguistic devices used effectively. • Discursive markers display extensive control.	• Continuous prose and paragraphs. • Paragraphs enhance meaning. • Structural features used appropriately. • Complex ideas are coherent.
Grade C *'clarity and success'*	• Communication is clear and shows clarity of thought, is successful. • Detailed, descriptive and informative ideas engage the reader. • Purpose and tone are appropriate. • Some linguistic devices such as rhetorical questions and hyperbole are used. • Discursive/informative markers such as 'furthermore' are used.	• Paragraphs in the whole text. • Some structural features used. • Well-thought-out ideas.
Grade F *'limited success'*	• Communicates a few ideas with limited success. • One or two ideas engage the reader in a limited way. • Awareness of purpose and intention is limited; ideas are very simple. • Linguistic devices may be attempted. • Limited vocabulary shows little use of informative markers.	• Erratic paragraphs. • Limited structural features used.

Task A

Write a letter to a friend explaining why you would like him or her to join you in a visit to a place you think is special.

Remember: you must refer to all parts of AO3 in your exam answer as they are all being tested: **communication, organisation, sentence structure, punctuation** and **spelling**.

Remember: the above table only accounts for 10/16 marks available for the shorter writing task and 16/24 marks in the longer writing task. The same table is used to assess both writing tasks. The remaining marks are awarded for accurate sentence structure, punctuation and spelling (see pages 51–56).

Student response to Task A

S. Winters

62 Brand New Lane

Uptown

Kent

KT2 5WH

Dear Chris,

I am writing to invite you to join me on a visit to our fabulous new house. It has been quite a while since I moved away from Liverpool and it would also be lovely to see you again.

You have to see it to believe it! There is everything I have always wished to have right here. We have a games room with its own full-sized snooker table; a darts board and even our own plasma screen for our Wii and Playstation. It is enormous! Who would not wish to live here? The sapphire blue swimming pool is indoors with a sliding roof and I have had professional swimming lessons and want to train for competitions on a national level.

Another great thing about moving here is the woods. They are a ten-minute walk away. There is a winding and sometimes scary pathway that I take as a short-cut. You can almost imagine it to be haunted by some spectacular ghost from generations ago…

Hope to see you soon.

Keep in touch,

Aidan

image DJ/Cadmium

Examiner's comment

The main ideas in this letter are presented successfully and they show clarity. The letter is informative and adopts an appropriate tone with the right degree of formality for an examination. Rhetorical devices are used. Paragraphs are used effectively and are of different lengths creating interest and variety. Ideas are expressed in well-thought-out sentences. If you read the Grade C descriptors, this would just about fulfil all of them.

Assessment for Learning

Identify evidence of the Grade C descriptors in the student response above. Discuss your findings with a partner. Did you identify the same things? Being able to identify the evidence of the grade descriptors in the letter will help you to use them and develop them further in your own writing.

Task B

Write a letter to a friend encouraging him or her to take up a fantastic new hobby that you discovered a short time ago.

Note: If your target grade is a C, you may use the beginning of the C-grade response below to start you off, substituting a hobby of your choice for go-karting.

Student response to Task B

> D. Ahmed
> 59 Old Lane
> Uxbridge
> London
> SE18 7AE
>
> Dear Pierre,
> I am writing to tell you about a fantastic new hobby I have taken up in here in Uxbridge. You will love it! I have taken up go-karting, once a fortnight. It is a real thrill and every time I go I just do not want it to end...

Nicola Gavin/Fotolia

Assessment for Learning

1 Assess your own work by identifying evidence of the A or C grade descriptors (depending on your target grade) in your letter.

2 Make a list of any you did not quite manage to include and use this as a target to improve the next letter or piece of writing you do.

3

AO3(iii): sentence structure, punctuation and spelling

Use a range of sentence structures for clarity, purpose and effect with accurate punctuation and spelling

How is AO3(iii) assessed?

Grade A	Grammatical structures and punctuation are used with success. Sentences are demarcated accurately. Sentence forms are used to good effect, including short sentences. Ambitious vocabulary is accurate.
Grade C	Your use of sentences and punctuation works well together. A variety of sentence forms is used. An increasingly developed vocabulary and accurate spelling of more common words are in evidence.
Grade F	Your use of sentences and punctuation shows some control. Sentence demarcation is sometimes accurate. Simple and complex sentences are used. Common words are accurately spelt. Standard English is used.

Refer back to the activities in Chapter 2 (pages 40–44) to develop your ability to write effective simple, compound and complex sentences. Skills you learn in one chapter or lesson must be applied elsewhere in your writing too if you are to become a successful and competent writer.

Punctuation

Punctuation is an important part of this AO. Students often make the mistake of thinking that punctuation is not significant as long as they have used it in their work. This is not the case. Accurate punctuation enhances meaning and gives more credibility and conviction to what you say because you are expressing it more effectively. Using punctuation accurately will therefore have more impact on your intended audience and gain you more marks. You need to practise using punctuation accurately all the time in all your work. It is not something that can be picked up with quick reference to a textbook; it is definitely a case of 'practice makes perfect' and you must make a conscious effort to improve and develop your use of it.

Key words	What the key words mean
accurate punctuation	Full stops and commas must be used accurately. You should know how putting a comma in a certain place helps to make meaning clear and can even enhance meaning. Accurate punctuation also includes the appropriate use of inverted commas for speech marks and quotations, exclamation marks and question marks. The confident Grade C and above student will also know how to use apostrophes, colons and semi-colons.

Task A

Most of the punctuation has been removed from this extract from an article in the *Telegraph* newspaper, highlighting the effects of knife crime. Rewrite the extract putting in the appropriate capital letters and punctuation.

Knife crime is a fact of life for teenagers

By Bryony Gordon

Before Ben sacks leaves school every day, he goes through a routine he removes his tie and blazer changes his shirt for a casual top and puts on different trousers the smart school shoes are replaced with trainers the final item he puts on is the most important the hoodie

But 14-year-old Ben is not part of a gang he isn't a feral youth with an ASBO quite the opposite he is a normal boy who wants to blend in so that he doesn't get mugged for a third time.

Ben talks about it all with a weariness that is alarming in one so young

The second time it happened there were nine of them, six of us we were walking home from football, and we had to go down an alley they followed us in and we knew what was going to happen so we started to run.

One of my mates stopped to ask a guy for help but he just said sorry I'm busy the group caught up with my friend and pushed him against railings took his wallet phone and his oyster travel card they started swearing at us saying that they were going to cut us through. Luckily, the gang dispersed.

Ingram

Assessment for Learning

1 Assess your own work by checking your use of punctuation. You can look the original article up at: **www.telegraph.co.uk/news/uknews/2055866/Knife-crime-is-a-fact-of-life-for-teenagers.html**

2 Practise punctuation by looking up newspaper articles on topics you are interested in, blanking out the punctuation, then adding it yourself before checking your work to see if you have added the punctuation correctly. (You could either cut and paste

your chosen articles into a blank document on your computer and complete the task there, maybe adding punctuation in a different colour so it stands out, or you could print the articles off and rewrite them by hand. You could even pair up with a friend and assess each other's work.)

Key words success ladder for AO3(iii)

	Sentence structure, punctuation and spelling (SSPS)
Grade A	• Punctuation and grammar are used with success. • Writing is organised, with sentences clearly demarcated. • A variety of sentence forms is used to good effect. • Ambitious vocabulary is used and spelt correctly. • Standard English is used appropriately.
Grade C	• Punctuation and grammar are used with control. • Writing is organised, with sentences mainly accurately demarcated. • A variety of sentence forms is used. • Spelling of commonly used words is accurate. • Standard English is used.
Grade F	• Punctuation and grammar are used with some control. • Writing is organised in sentences which are sometimes accurately demarcated. • Simple and complex sentences are used. • Ambitious vocabulary is used and spelt correctly. • Standard English is used appropriately.

Task B

Write an article for a teenage magazine, highlighting the dangers and worries about knife crime.

Remember: the focus, apart from the content of your answer, should be your use of punctuation.

Student response to Task B

I think knife crime is happening more often most teenagers I think have had enough and its time we put a stop to it all teenagers deserve to feel safe on the streets of their home town we should not have to walk around trying to protect ourselves against attacks from teenagers.

Examiner's comment

The main problem with this student's work is a very common one: there is a lack of full stops. The work is in sentences, but the student has clearly not remembered to add full stops in the appropriate places. You can lose crucial marks if you do not pay attention to this when you write. This would just about fulfil the punctuation requirements for Grade F.

1 Rewrite the above student response to Task B, putting in the correct punctuation marks.

2 Now check your answer against the improved version below.

Student response to Task B

Improved version

I think knife crime is happening more often. Most teenagers, I think, have had enough and it's time we put a stop to it all! Teenagers deserve to feel safe on the streets of their home town. We should not have to walk around trying to protect ourselves against attacks from teenagers.

Examiner's comment

This student's work now contains appropriate punctuation. The work is now in clearly demarcated sentences and the student has remembered to add full stops, apostrophes and an exclamation mark in the appropriate places. If you read the Grade C descriptors, this would now fulfil the punctuation element for this grade.

Assessment for Learning

Write two paragraphs about stopping knife crime and check your use of punctuation matches the grade descriptors for your target grade. You may continue the student example above or write a new response of your own.

> *Remember:* one of the biggest barriers to gaining a C grade or above in the punctuation element of the exam is not using full stops and apostrophes accurately. Make sure you develop your skills in these to a good standard.

Conjunctions

Using conjunctions effectively can help you improve the sentence structure, punctuation and spelling element of your written exam and controlled writing assessments. Conjunctions *connect* or *link* the words, phrases or clauses in a sentence. There are three main types of conjunctions:

coordinating conjunctions

subordinating conjunctions

correlative conjunctions

It is important to select the right types of conjunctions to use in the appropriate places in your writing.

Coordinating conjunctions

These link grammatically equal words and word groups. They must always join similar elements, e.g. subject + subject, verb (phrase) + verb (phrase), noun (phrase) + noun (phrase), sentence + sentence.

Conjunction	What it links	Example	Your own example
but	subject + subject	Daniyal loves computer games but Sophia loves books.	
or	verb (phrase) + verb (phrase)	Did you hear or see the commotion outside yesterday?	
and	noun (phrase) + noun (phrase)	I have tickets for the coach and the train.	
so	sentence + sentence	I wanted to stay over at my friend's house so I finished all my homework.	

Task C

Copy and complete this table of coordinating conjunctions, adding your own examples in the final column.

Assessment for Learning

1 Underline the different parts of the links in the same colours, e.g. subject + subject, in your own examples.

2 Try to create your own examples from scratch. Experiment with using different conjunctions to link different types. For example, try linking a verb + verb with 'and'. This will help you learn about when and how conjunctions work and making the right choices in your own writing.

Correlative conjunctions

These are word pairs that link grammatically equal words and word groups. They connect sentence elements of the same kind and are different from coordinating conjunctions in that they are always used in pairs.

Conjunction	What it links	Example	Your own example
both...and	subject + subject	**Both** Andrew **and** Jo were hilarious on stage.	
neither...nor	verb (phrase) + verb (phrase)	**Neither** dancing **nor** swimming seemed appealing today.	
either...or	noun (phrase) + noun (phrase)	We could visit **either** a castle **or** a football ground.	
not only... but also	sentence + sentence	**Not only** did I finish the exam **but** I **also** came top of the class.	

Task D

Copy and complete the table of correlative conjunctions above, adding your own examples in the final column.

Subordinating conjunctions

These begin adverb clauses and link them to independent clauses. They connect subordinate clauses to a main clause.

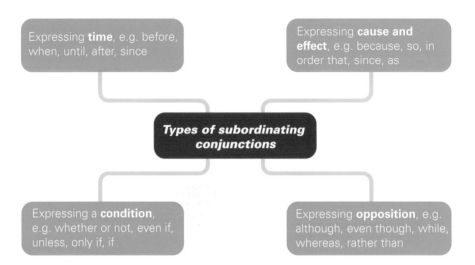

Expressing **time**, e.g. before, when, until, after, since

Expressing **cause and effect**, e.g. because, so, in order that, since, as

Types of subordinating conjunctions

Expressing a **condition**, e.g. whether or not, even if, unless, only if, if

Expressing **opposition**, e.g. although, even though, while, whereas, rather than

Conjunction	Example	Your own example
before	I have to finish my homework **before** I can go out.	
because	Alison cannot go out in the garden **because** she is afraid of spiders.	
whereas	Tom is a keen swimmer **whereas** I prefer mountain trekking.	
unless	You cannot stay out late at the party **unless** you have a friend to walk home with.	

Task E

Copy and complete the table of subordinating conjunctions above, adding your own examples in the final column.

Unit 1: longer writing task

The longer writing task is worth 24 marks in Section B of the Unit 1 paper in both the Higher and Foundation Tiers. You will need to refer to the tables earlier in this chapter for the assessment criteria for communication, organisation, sentence structure, punctuation and spelling as all of the above apply to the written tasks in this part of the examination too.

Task A

Animal rights campaigners argue that it is cruel to keep wild animals in small, confined spaces such as zoos and that they should be left free to roam in their natural habitats.

Write an article for a newspaper which argues for or against this idea.

Student response to Task A

Most places in England have at least one zoo, which will be visited by many thousands of people every year. For many, this is a positive experience as well as a long-lasting memory. Many animals are born in zoos and don't know any different so it cannot be classed as cruelty.

Animal rights organisations may say that keeping animals in zoos is cruel and should not be allowed. However, many children would not get to see such animals if they were not kept in a zoo. I would not even know what a giraffe or a lion really looked like if it had not been for my visits to my local zoo. How did you feel on your first visit to the zoo as a child? I have seen children's faces light up when they have seen such fascinating animals which seem happy and content in their surroundings…

Examiner's comment

This student's point of view is communicated with success. There is evidence of a clear thought process and childhood memories of visiting the zoo are clearly stated. Ideas are persuasively presented and the tone of the article is appropriately serious. Discourse markers such as 'however' are used. Emotive language, such as the reference to the 'children's faces' lighting up, impacts successfully on the reader. Paragraphs are effective and ideas are well presented in sentences. If you read the Grade C descriptors for AO3(i) (communication) and AO3(ii) (organisation), this response would just about fulfil all the criteria.

In addition, sentences, punctuation and spelling are controlled. Vocabulary is developed. A range of punctuation is used. Standard English is used appropriately. This would fulfil the criteria for Grade C in AO3(iii).

Assessment for Learning

1 Continue the student response above.
2 Assess your own work by highlighting where you meet the A or C grade criteria (depending on your target grade) for AO3(i)–(iii).
3 Redraft your work, improving it to make sure you fulfil any A or C grade criteria you did not meet in your original version.

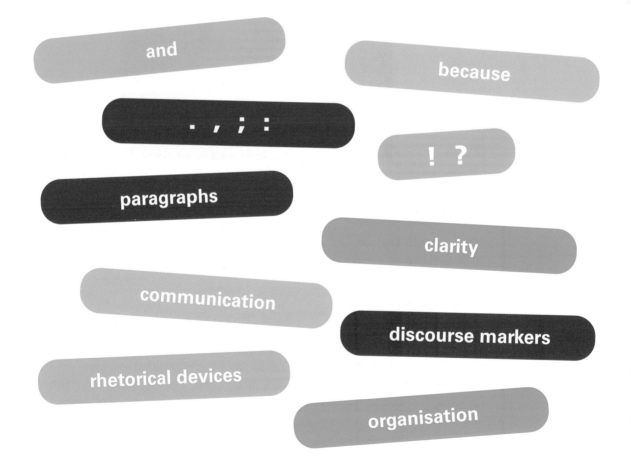

B Writing

Chapter 4

Writing formats

We all experience different writing formats in our everyday lives: the charity leaflet through the door, the newspaper we buy, the review we read for the film we want to watch at the cinema etc. The examinations and assessments in GCSE English and English Language require that you can recognise and write in a range of different key formats. You should consider these to be like formulae or the frames within which you write. For example, if you are asked to write a letter or an article in the exam, you need to know what makes a successful letter or article.

You might ask: why do I need to learn how to write an article or a review, for example? This is because in your everyday life, you will come across situations where you will probably read them and maybe even be influenced by them. You need to understand how they are created, what their purpose is and be able to interpret them and distinguish between the bias elements so that you can reach your own independent conclusions. Writing non-fiction successfully, especially letters, is an important functional skill in life.

This chapter is designed to give you an insight into the main features of the key writing formats and provide you with the opportunity to use them in your own writing. The features list for each format is not exhaustive and your teacher may point out additional ones.

Try to learn the features of each writing format, practise listing them and creating examples of your own in response to examination questions or tasks you have created. It would also be a good idea to start collecting real-life examples of writing formats as you come across them — try to highlight and label their key features. Focus on the formats you have had less opportunity to develop or are the least confident in tackling.

The key writing formats we are going to look at in this chapter are shown below.

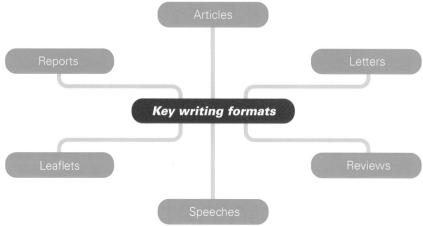

AO3

For GCSE English, your writing will be assessed against the following Assessment Objectives (AOs) in both Units 1 and 3. The key words are emboldened. These were explained in Chapter 2 (pages 36, 38 and 40). Note that at least one third of the available marks will be allocated to AO3(iii).

AO3(i)	• **Communicate clearly** and **imaginatively**, **using**, **adapting** and **selecting vocabulary** appropriate to task and purpose in ways that engage the reader.
AO3(ii)	• **Organise** information and ideas into **structured** and **sequenced** sentences, paragraphs and whole texts, using a variety of **linguistic structural features** to support **cohesion** and overall **coherence**.
AO3(iii)	• Use a range of **sentence structures** for **clarity, purpose** and **effect** with **accurate punctuation** and **spelling**.

This Assessment Objective, AO3, is known as AO4 in the English Language specifications. The content is exactly the same and for ease of reference and to avoid confusion, it is mainly referred to as AO3 in this book.

For more information about where and how AO3 is assessed refer back to Chapters 2 and 3.

4

General grade criteria for writing in English and English Language

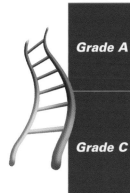

Grade A	Candidates show a confident and assured control over a range of forms and styles and these are appropriate to different tasks and purposes. Texts written are engaging and hold the reader's interest throughout through logical arguments, persuasive force or creative delight; these are very important aspects and qualities of A-grade writing.
Grade C	Candidates successfully adapt their writing to the required forms and styles for different tasks and purposes. Texts are written which engage the reader's interest. The structure of the text is supported by effective paragraphs which make the sequence of events and development of ideas coherent. A range of varied sentence structures is used to create different effects. Vocabulary choices are varied. Punctuation and spelling are accurate.
Grade F	Candidates' writing shows some adaptation to the required forms and styles for the task and purpose. Texts are written which communicate simply and clearly with the reader. The structure of the text contains events which are logically sequenced. Paragraphs are straightforward and effective. Sentence structures, including some that are complex, are usually correct. Vocabulary is sometimes chosen for variety and interest. Basic punctuation and spelling are mostly accurate.

Remember: A-grade writers show a confident and assured control over what they write every step of the way. C-grade candidates adapt their writing successfully to the different forms and purposes but have not mastered the control exhibited by an A-grade writer. F-grade candidates manage to adapt some of what they are writing and communicate simply and clearly with the reader.

Reports

Headings

Appropriate audience

Clarity

Appropriate tone

Information

Organisation: introduction, conclusion, recommendations

Task A

Find an example of a report on the internet and try to imitate its style in writing your own report.

Remember: you also write reports in school in your science experiments. Look back at one you have done and identify the format features for a report.

Articles

Catchy title, often with a pun (play on words)

Caption

Clear first paragraph

Three or four content paragraphs

Photograph related to the article (do not draw, write a one-line description in the space)

Charts, diagrams etc. (indicate where these would go, but do not draw)

Short and clear summary

Task A

Read the article below and identify evidence/use of the above features in it.

Mississippi madness

Travel chaos struck drivers when this bridge across the Mississippi started to creak and its concrete pillars collapsed

The motorway bridge was one of the most used stretches of road across the Mississippi in Minneapolis. Over 140,000 vehicles crossed it each day. An even expanse of concrete, it didn't even look like a bridge.

There were no high towers or suspension cables. Yet its smooth surface was hiding a tragedy waiting to happen. The effects of corrosion, the weight of all the traffic and the weather had gradually eroded the bridge's structure.

On Wednesday 1 August at the height of the rush hour it gave way.

TopFoto

Assessment for Learning

Cut out two newspaper articles. Stick them into your book and identify the features of this writing format, the article. Use these to write your own examples and ask a friend to see if they can identify the obvious features in the articles you have created.

Letters

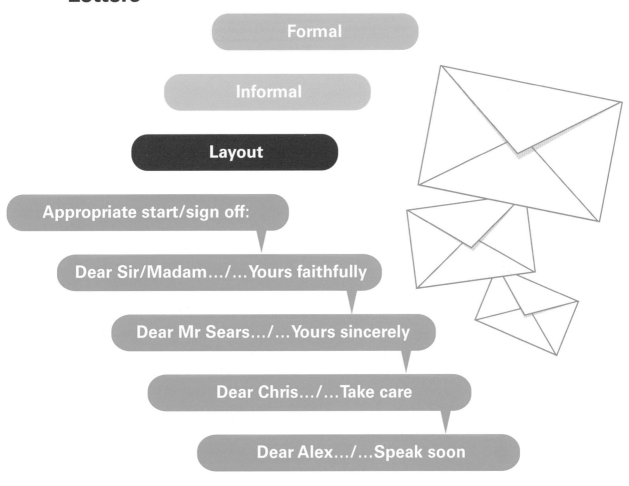

Formal

Informal

Layout

Appropriate start/sign off:

Dear Sir/Madam…/…Yours faithfully

Dear Mr Sears…/…Yours sincerely

Dear Chris…/…Take care

Dear Alex…/…Speak soon

Katie Cartwright

49 Bristol Close

Banks

Birmingham

B22 3JC

Councillor T. Reeves

333 Robin Drive

Banks

Birmingham

B22 5JC

Dear Councillor Reeves

I am writing to express my concerns over the growing levels of anti-social behaviour in my local area. As a resident of Banks for 20 years, I have never known things to be so bad. I feel I am living my life in fear of reprisals from teenagers who are just out of control and out of touch with how people are feeling about their behaviour.

Many members of the local community feel as strongly as I do. A lot of trouble has been caused by teenagers who are joyriding in cars very much under the wrong impression that scaring residents, especially children, is cool. Only last week a child was quite seriously injured as he ran away frightened from one such car, straight into a side street without looking, where another car was speeding past. Extremely frightening! Does something more serious need to happen to make the council do something to stop this? We have complained so many times but no one seems to listen…

I look forward to hearing from you as a matter of urgency.

Yours sincerely

K. Cartwright

(Ms Katie Cartwright)

Assessment for Learning

Before you read the examiner's comment below, identify the format features this student has used successfully. Point out and correct the ones this student has not quite managed to develop.

Examiner's comment

This student has used the required format of writing a formal letter, using formal language. The text itself is interesting and engaging and the reference to the incident involving a child at danger from a joy-rider gives the letter substance and a sense of reality.

The structure is supported by effective, varied paragraphs, containing coherent ideas. Vocabulary is varied and punctuation and spelling are correct and accurate. This fulfils the writing criteria for a Grade C.

Assessment for Learning

1 Imagine you are a teenager who has read this letter in your local newspaper. Using the Grade C criteria in the 'Key words success ladder for AO3(i) and AO3(ii)' on page 48, write a Grade C formal letter as a response, in role, as a teenager who is upset by this damaging view of what seems to be all teenagers.

2 Read through your letter and draw arrows to highlight and label where you think you have met the Grade C criteria. Set yourself a target, highlighting one thing you need to improve. Address this in your next attempt.

3 Once you are confident you can do this, try to redraft your letter to meet the Grade A criteria in the 'Key words success ladder for AO3(i) and AO3(ii)' on page 48.

Leaflets

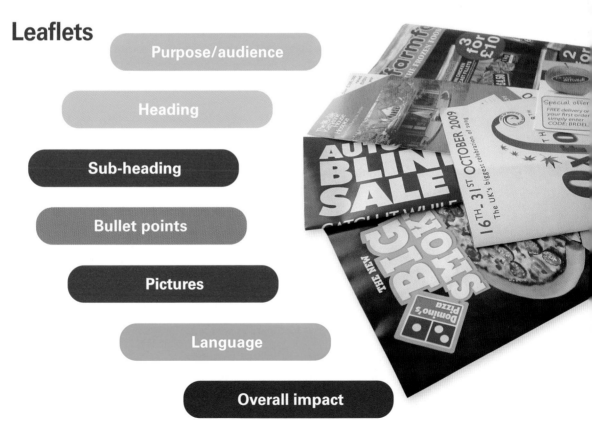

Purpose/audience

Heading

Sub-heading

Bullet points

Pictures

Language

Overall impact

You will have many leaflets posted through your door, maybe even given out at school. Collect these and make a list of common and uncommon features. You may even spot some new features. You can view many different types of leaflets on the internet too.

Speeches

The rhetorical devices listed on page 75 in Chapter 5 are vital in writing speeches and persuasive texts. Refer to these to help you write your answers to the tasks in this section.

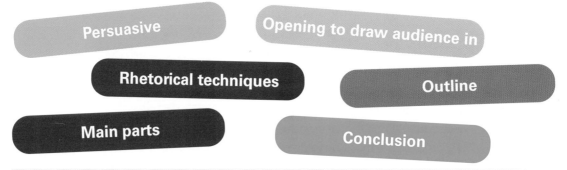

Persuasive

Opening to draw audience in

Rhetorical techniques

Outline

Main parts

Conclusion

Task A

Write a speech opposing the view that most young people are involved in anti-social behaviour. The speech is to be given at a meeting of the local community and students from the area.

Student response to Task A

Ladies and gentleman, fellow students, welcome to today's meeting about anti-social behaviour.

I would like to begin this speech by pointing out that not all teenagers are involved in anti-social behaviour. In fact, they suffer at the hands of the very society in which we live. You may ask why that is. It is the same question other students from local schools and I have been asking of ourselves.

We are not all the terrible vicious vandals that the press would have you believe. We are not crazy bullies you have to confront on every street corner. No we are not!

At every opportunity given to us, many of us have raised money for local charities such as Cancer Research and children who have to spend their time in hospices, who are not as fortunate as we are...

Examiner's comment

This student has used the format of a speech successfully and included some rhetorical devices such as repetition, emotive language and forceful phrases. The speech is successful in its purpose and makes the reader consider how teenagers are presented in the media.

Paragraphs are used effectively and spelling and punctuation is accurate. This fulfils the writing criteria for a Grade C.

Assessment for Learning

Continue this speech for another three paragraphs. Try to include at least three new rhetorical devices that have not been used in it so far. When you have finished writing, either underline the rhetorical devices you have used yourself or swap with a friend and see if you can identify them in each other's work. Check you have used them correctly. Make any necessary corrections.

Reviews

Keep the reader's interest

Some detail...but should not give too much away

Often about films, plays, books, shows etc.

Lively, engaging

Task A

1 Read this review of the film, *The Poison Chalice*. Pick out the key features of a review.
2 Write a review of your own favourite film in the same style. Refer back to the general criteria for writing in English and English Language on page 61 to remind yourself of what is required.

Review

The Poison Chalice
☆ ☆ ☆ ☆ ☆

This is a film for the whole family, though if you are an older viewer, the plot is a little simplistic on occasions. The band of brothers fight just a little too readily but the quest for immortality is portrayed brilliantly, encapsulating both suspense and entertainment while holding the viewer's interest. Ganronde, the protagonist, half-man,

half machine, has powers which have developed since the prequel and his band of followers, the brothers, are enslaved to him after he saves their lives.

Set in the year 2090, the journey that the men go on, after drinking from the chalice, leads them through new lands and their meeting with Ganronde's mother, Dinessa, in the land of dreams is quite moving, as we learn of his desire to avenge his father's death at the hands of humankind who existed many moons ago.

As the plot develops, it does become much more complex and intriguing. This is a film that will take you to the edge of your seat as secrets are revealed and each man in the band of brothers experiences poisonous revelations about their lives, leaving us asking questions about our own...

Extract from a film review for *The Poison Chalice*, 2011 release, by Zakki Matthew.

Vuk Vukmirovic/Fotolia

Assessment for Learning

Look back at the general criteria for writing in English and English Language on page 61 and check which ones your answer meets. Have you written an A or C grade answer?

You can use the checklist below to help you check if you have met the C-grade criteria. Check you:

- Adapt your writing to the required format.   ☐
- Engage the reader.   ☐
- Use effective paragraphs.   ☐
- Sequence ideas and events coherently.   ☐
- Use a range of varied paragraphs.   ☐
- Vary vocabulary choices.   ☐
- Use accurate spelling and punctuation.   ☐

Highlight and label where each of these requirements is met in your work.

And finally...

Familiarise yourself with the different writing forms and formats. Learn the different styles for each writing format. Consider **form**, **audience**, **purpose** and **tone** in your writing. These are the 'tools' that prepare you for writing well.

Practise writing in a range of different formats. Create questions of your own to practise what you have learned. Plan and answer them in timed conditions. Discover what your strengths and weaknesses as a writer are, set personal targets and focus on improving these areas in your work.

Writing is like any other craft: master the key skills and you are well on the way to being an engaging and successful writer.

B

Writing

Chapter 5

Writing styles and purposes

Being able to write in an appropriate style for a range of purposes, to argue, persuade, advise, inform, explain and describe, is an important life skill. Once you start to take responsibility for yourself, living away from home and earning your own living, you will find that there will be times when you need to voice an opinion or concern in a manner that allows you to be heard. You will want what you say to be effective and your point of view to be respected. This is why we teach you such skills in school, to allow you to be independent and to be able to stand up for yourself in a way that is acceptable in society.

Think about some situations where writing skills of this kind might be useful:

- arguing against what you consider to be an unfair parking fine
- arguing against the building of a drug rehabilitation centre in your local area
- persuading people to give to a charity close to your heart because someone you know has suffered
- campaigning for human rights
- persuading the local police to do something about anti-social behaviour in your area

- arguing against animal cruelty
- advising a friend in a letter about problems he/she is having at home
- informing teenagers about how to take up a hobby by writing a leaflet or website about it
- explaining why the road where you live needs repairing in a letter to your local council
- describing how an accident happened in an insurance claim

Can you think of any others? List three or four more.

For GCSE English, your writing will be assessed against the following Assessment Objectives (AOs) in both Units 1 and 3. The key words are emboldened; these were explained in Chapter 2 (pages 36, 38 and 40). Note that at least one third of the available marks will be allocated to AO3(iii).

AO3(i)	• **Communicate clearly** and **imaginatively**, **using**, **adapting** and **selecting vocabulary** appropriate to task and purpose in ways that engage the reader.
AO3(ii)	• **Organise** information and ideas into **structured** and **sequenced** sentences, paragraphs and whole texts, using a variety of **linguistic structural features** to support **cohesion** and overall **coherence**.
AO3(iii)	• Use a range of **sentence structures** for **clarity, purpose** and **effect** with **accurate punctuation** and **spelling**.

This Assessment Objective, AO3, is known as AO4 in the English Language specifications. The content is exactly the same and for ease of reference and to avoid confusion, it is mainly referred to as AO3 in this book.

For more information about where and how AO3 is assessed refer back to Chapters 2 and 3.

Writing to argue

Just like any good recipe there are certain ingredients that you need to create a good and effective text which is well structured. You may not always 'win' real-life arguments on serious issues but you can make a real difference by making your views heard and at least making people listen and pay attention to them. Part of living in a democracy is our right to speak freely about issues that concern us. On the opposite page is a suggested structure to use when writing to argue.

Introduction: write an introduction showing your understanding of the question and communicating your intentions.

Argument: link the intention you stated and expand this into your first well-thought-out point of view giving a reason.

Counter-argument: present a counter-argument, including a reason. This shows you understand the opposing point of view.

Argument: write another argument supporting your point of view and giving a reason.

Counter-argument: present a counter-argument, including a reason. Again, be certain it does not overpower your own strong arguments.

Argument: write another argument supporting your point of view and giving a reason.

Counter-argument: present a counter-argument, including a reason. Again, be certain it does not overpower your own strong arguments.

Conclusion: write a conclusion summing up the key points in your argument. It should clearly try to persuade the reader that your argument is the one that should be supported.

Task A

Write an argument against keeping and using animals in circus performances.

Joël Dallio/Fotolia

Remember: follow the suggested structure above. Refer to all parts of AO3 in your answer as they are all being tested: **communication, organisation, sentence structure, punctuation** and **spelling.**

Student response to Task A

Student answer 1

Everyone in it has rights, both human beings and animals. The circus seems to be a happy place. We saw this as children. Now that we are adults; we need to think about animal cruelty. Is it right to keep animals in cages? I would argue that it is not.

All they see are the bars of their cages and claustrophobic cells with little or no exercise. Animals are often overworked so that people can earn a living. We must ask ourselves 'at what cost?' Animal welfare should come first.

On the other hand, some people might say children may never get to see animals close up. But there are wildlife safari parks which have more open spaces…

Examiner's comment

The main ideas in this argument are clear and successfully conveyed. It contains some informative ideas that engage interest. The tone is appropriate and there is some successful use of rhetorical devices such as a rhetorical question and some use of emotive language that impacts on the reader. Paragraphs and discourse markers are used and there is a sense of structure to this answer. A better developed vocabulary and more developed ideas would improve this answer, which is currently a C-grade response.

Note this candidate has not made use of a plan and this is always recommended.

Assessment for Learning

Complete the above answer, keeping in mind the advice given in the examiner's comment. Identify the features you have improved by labelling these in your work.

Student response to Task A

Student answer 2

Plan

> **Introduction**: human rights…animal cruelty…caged animals.

> **Argument**: claustrophobic conditions. No freedom. Overworked in captivity

> **Counter-argument**: Children never see close up…but safari parks are available…

Answer

Our society has brought us up to believe that everyone in it has rights; that includes human beings and animals. The 'happy' circus performances we may

Wichittra Srisunon/Fotolia

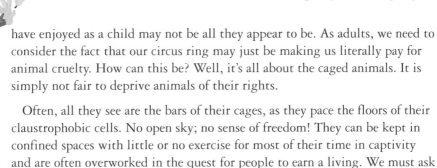

have enjoyed as a child may not be all they appear to be. As adults, we need to consider the fact that our circus ring may just be making us literally pay for animal cruelty. How can this be? Well, it's all about the caged animals. It is simply not fair to deprive animals of their rights.

Often, all they see are the bars of their cages, as they pace the floors of their claustrophobic cells. No open sky; no sense of freedom! They can be kept in confined spaces with little or no exercise for most of their time in captivity and are often overworked in the quest for people to earn a living. We must ask ourselves 'at what cost?' Animal welfare should come before financial welfare.

On the other hand, some people might argue that children may never get to see animals close up. But there are wildlife safari parks which provide a far more natural environment than circuses and zoos…

Examiner's comment

The main ideas in this answer are convincing and compelling. It contains detailed, well-thought-out ideas which convince the reader that the writer's point of view is correct or influential at the very least. The purpose of the text is clearly defined and expressed and the use of discursive markers is controlled. Paragraphs enhance meaning and the structural features are effective. This candidate has planned his/her answer and this is evident. This candidate would get a Grade A for this answer if the rest of it continued in the same manner.

Task B

Argue the case against the building of a drugs rehabilitation centre in your local area.

Try to write a Grade A or C response, depending on your target grade. Refer back to the general grade criteria for writing in Chapter 4 (page 61) to see what is required for each grade.

Remember: use the planning structure and keep referring to the writing criteria for your target grade to help you structure your answer. Planning is a crucial part of writing a well-structured response.

Assessment for Learning

Assess your work against the general grade criteria for writing on page 61 to see if you have achieved your target grade. You may find some of your writing falls into different grades; this is quite normal. It is up to you to set yourself targets to see what you need to do to move your weaker areas up into the higher grades. The more self- and peer-assessment you do, the easier this will become.

Writing to persuade

The emphasis of this type of writing is to use good points and arguments to **persuade** your reader or audience to go along with your point of view and, more importantly, this type of writing can 'spur people into taking action'. Charities wanting to raise money often rely on this type of writing. Debates and speeches on sensitive or controversial issues, such as speeches about abortion or organ donation, are more effective when a persuasive tone is used, supported by arguments if appropriate, which are well thought out.

In order to persuade and argue effectively there are two key things that you need to develop your skills in: using rhetorical devices and discourse markers. Discourse markers are words or phrases that allow you to communicate the structure of your writing to the reader, for example 'first', 'second', 'in addition', 'I think', 'in other words'.

Rhetorical devices

Believe it or not, you are probably quite an expert at using some of these already, even though you may not realise it. You are probably quite good at 'getting your own way'. How many times have you had to persuade people around you to do certain things? For example, convincing adults to let you have that very late night, to stay out at that all night party or to buy you that wonderfully expensive outfit you have just seen that is going to make you stand out from the crowd. Well, think about the things you might say in situations such as these, emphasising and repeating points, trying to get someone to see them your way. You might say:

> 'Oh, please, please, I've got to have that pair of jeans! I'll just die of embarrassment if I have to wear those old, scruffy ones. Oh, come on, you don't want me to look like I can't afford to get a new pair, do you?'

The above 'plea' uses things like **repetition, pronouns, exclamation, emotive language** and **plays on the reader's sympathy**. All of these are **rhetorical devices**. In effect, you are using the art of rhetoric. So you see, you are more of an expert than you might have thought!

Using rhetorical devices

Rhetoric is the art of writing and speaking effectively and using words impressively. At times it can involve artificial and exaggerated language. **Rhetorical devices** are the techniques, or things, we use to enhance what we are saying or writing.

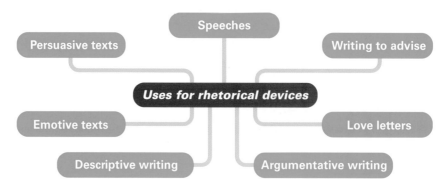

The art of 'speaking' to an audience, be that verbal or written, is something we will do all our lives. So, effective communication skills are a great thing to have. We can use rhetorical devices to support, enhance and emphasise what we are trying to say or write and to maximise its impact on our intended audience. The diagram opposite gives some examples of where it would be appropriate to use rhetorical devices. Can you think of any others?

The following diagram lists many possible rhetorical devices.

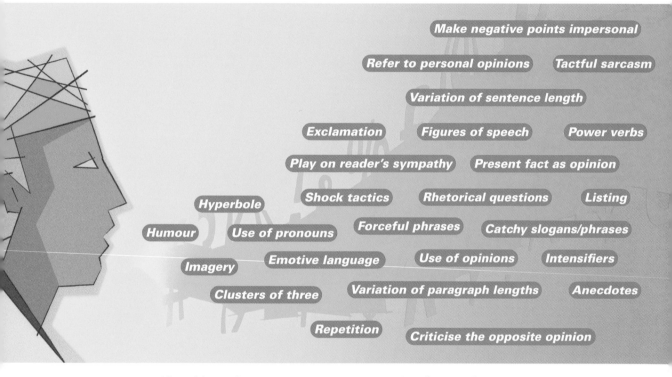

The table on the next two pages gives examples of many of the rhetorical devices listed above. Every speech may not contain every rhetorical device; the art of rhetoric includes being able to select which devices are effective and will have an impact on your intended audience and purpose.

Task A

1 Study the table carefully. Try to identify examples of each rhetorical device as you read examples of speeches from this textbook, examples given to you by your teacher or examples that you have found on the internet.

2 Copy and complete the table by adding examples of your own in the final column.

Remember: when you are asked to write your own speeches you could try selecting the rhetorical devices you would like to use and creating a table like the one on pages 76–77 so that you can fill in well-thought-out examples you can add to your speech.

Rhetorical device	Example	Your own example
Rhetorical questions	Can we accept such behaviour?	
Repetition	'…I have a dream that my four little children will one day live in a nation where they will not be judged by the colour of their skin but by the content of their character. I have a dream today!'[1]	
Imagery	'… we will not be satisfied until "justice rolls down like waters, and righteousness like a mighty stream"'[1]	
Play on reader's sympathy	'I stand before you today the representative of a family in grief, in a country in mourning before a world in shock…'[2]	
Variation of sentence lengths	'…And here we come to another truth about her. For all the status, the glamour, the applause, Diana remained throughout a very insecure person at heart, almost childlike in her desire to do good for others so she could release herself from deep feelings of unworthiness of which her eating disorders were merely a symptom…'[2]	
Emotive language	'…your quest…quest for freedom left you battered by the storms of persecution and staggered by the winds of police brutality.'[1]	
Use of pronouns	'…We will all feel cheated that you were taken from us so young and yet we must learn to be grateful that you came along at all…'[2]	
Rule of three	'Friends, Romans, Countrymen'[4]	
Criticise the opposite opinion	'It is a tragic mix-up when the United States spends $500,000 for every enemy soldier killed, and only $53 annually on the victims of poverty.'[3]	
Hyperbole	'…There is a temptation to rush to canonise your memory…'[2]	
Use of opinions	'…I don't think she ever understood why her genuinely good intentions were sneered at by the media…'[2]	

Rhetorical device	Example	Your own example
Presentation of fact as opinion	The most beautiful woman in the world.	
Humour	'I was obliged to excuse the chairman from introducing me, because he never compliments anybody and I knew I could do it just as well.'[6]	
Exclamation	'I have a dream today!'[1]	
Power verbs	'…We can never be satisfied as long as our children are stripped of their self-hood and robbed of their dignity…'[1]	
Forceful phrases	'You have been the veterans of creative suffering.'[1]	
Catchy slogans/ phrases	'…I have a dream…'[1]	
Figures of speech	'I want to give people who are cruel to animals a piece of my mind.'	
Tactful sarcasm	'…the Emancipation Proclamation… came as a joyous daybreak to end the long night of their captivity. But one hundred years later, the Negro still is not free.'[3]	
Intensifiers	'…we want you to know that life without you is very, very difficult.'[2]	
Anecdotes	'…I would rather cherish the days I spent with her in March when she came to visit me and my children in our home in South Africa…'[2]	
Make negative points impersonal	'…a girl given the name of the ancient goddess of hunting was, in the end, the most hunted person of the modern age.'[2]	
Shock tactics	'Cigarettes killed my…but still I started smoking'.[5]	

1 Martin Luther King's speech, 'I Have A Dream'
2 Earl Spencer's funeral oration in memory of Princess Diana, reproduced by kind permission of the Earl Spencer
3 Martin Luther King
4 Speech in the play *Julius Caesar* by William Shakespeare
5 Patrick Reynolds' Keynote Address on World No Tobacco Day before the United Nations' Child Health 2000 Congress
6 Mark Twain's 'Our Fellow Savages', humorous speech in 1866

Why are rhetorical devices effective?

In speech, for example in everyday conversation, we enhance our rhetoric by using gestures and adopting appropriate facial expressions. Our body language will often complement the information or messages we are trying to communicate. In a telephone conversation, we might use voice, tone and intonation to express what we are trying to say effectively. We do not have this luxury in our writing.

Rhetorical devices establish relationships between a communicator and his or her intended audience. By using rhetorical devices, we can manipulate language and make what we want to say more effective.

Who uses rhetorical devices?

Politicians, animal rights' activists, people campaigning for changes in the law and even the media use rhetorical devices to try to get us to see things their way. You and I might use them to convince people when we are arguing our point of view. We need these skills, not just in the exams but as we come across situations throughout our lives. For example, we might use rhetorical devices in a wedding speech or a funeral oration when we are sharing our memories with relatives and friends. Being able to say what you want to say in a way that reaches the widest possible audience, as occasion demands, is a life-long skill that you will hopefully continue to develop with experience.

You can use rhetoric on happy, sad, serious and even humorous occasions.

Rhetoric in practice: Princess Diana's funeral

Great speakers are known as *orators* and they use rhetorical devices in their speeches. Earl Spencer (Princess Diana's brother and Prince William's uncle) made a moving funeral oration in memory of his sister. This speech is rich with rhetorical devices as were the headlines surrounding the occasion. Before we go on to the speech itself, we are going to study some of the headlines reported on Princess Diana's funeral.

A Nation Mourns
As the world looks on,
Britain buries a princess

The Funeral:
A Final Farewell

**Tearful
Farewell**

Task B

1 What do you notice about the language used in the headlines on the opposite page? Which of the rhetorical devices can you spot? One example is the use of emotive words that also play on the reader's sympathy, such as the idea that the farewell is 'tearful'. Most people can associate with this and feel a sense of empathy.

2 Write five alternative headlines that are equally effective using the same rhetorical devices.

Task C

Look up the full text of Earl Spencer's speech on the internet and read it aloud to yourself so you get a real sense of its power and impact. Listen to an audio version.

We are now going to study some parts of this funeral oration in detail. Read the following extract:

TopFoto

Earl Spencer speaking at the funeral

'I stand before you today the representative of a family in grief, in a country in mourning, before a world in shock.

We are all united not only in our desire to pay our respects to Diana but rather in our need to do so...

For such was her extraordinary appeal that tens of millions of people taking part in this service all over the world...who never actually met her, feel that they too lost someone close to them in the early hours of Sunday morning. It is a more remarkable tribute to Diana than I can ever hope to offer her today...'

Task D

1 In the opening two lines which rhetorical devices can you identify? Try to find at least two.
2 a Underline the pronouns in the extract, for example 'we', which help to establish a direct link with the audience.
  b Who is the audience?
  c Why do you think Earl Spencer uses such pronouns? Consider the purpose of the speech.
3 a List all the emotive words used in the extract.
  b Use a thesaurus to try to find alternative words. Substitute them for the originals in the extract and read it back to yourself. How successful is your choice of words?

Earl Spencer goes on to describe Princess Diana's character and what she meant to others around her:

TopFoto

Princess Diana

'Diana was the very essence of compassion, of duty, of style, of beauty. All over the world she was the symbol of selfless humanity, a standard-bearer for the rights of the truly downtrodden, a truly British girl who transcended nationality, someone with a natural nobility who was classless, who proved in the last year that she needed no royal title to generate her particular brand of magic…

Today is our chance to say "thank you" for the way you brightened our lives…'

Task E

Identify four of the qualities Earl Spencer says Diana had. Are these facts or opinions? How do you know?

Remember: you are also asked about fact and opinions in the reading section of the exam.

Diana was stripped of her title when she and Prince Charles divorced. Why do you think Earl Spencer makes reference to the royal title she once had. What is the purpose of this reference?

Towards the end of the speech, Earl Spencer addresses Princes William and Harry personally:

'William and Harry, we all care desperately for you two today. We are all chewed up with sadness at the loss of a woman who wasn't even our mother. How great your suffering is we cannot even imagine.'

Then he goes on to address a wider audience:

'I would like to end by thanking God for the small mercies he has shown us at this dreadful time; for taking Diana at her most beautiful and radiant and when she had so much joy in her private life.

Above all, we give thanks for the life of a woman I am so proud to be able to call my sister: the unique, the complex, the extraordinary and irreplaceable Diana, whose beauty, both internal and external, will never be extinguished from our minds.'

Extracts reproduced by kind permission of the Earl Spencer

Note how many different audiences he addresses here. What purpose do you think he has in mind? Identify the rhetorical devices Earl Spencer uses to achieve his purpose.

Rhetoric in practice: over to you

Now it is time to have a go at being rhetorical yourself. This will enable you to check how well you have understood the key ideas and show you what you still need to revise and improve.

Task F

Write an opening for a speech persuading someone to donate money to your favourite charity. This should be about two to three paragraphs.

Student response to Task F

I stand here today, ladies and gentlemen, to invite you to donate to a worthy cause: Cancer Research. Cancer is an illness that has probably affected either someone close to us or someone we know of from a friend or an acquaintance. So, we know only too well that it can affect a patient's life or the lives of their loved ones for years to come. Ladies and gentlemen, we all know that cancer can be a killer and without Cancer Research many more lives would have been affected, devastated and even lost. I ask you to give generously to an organisation that helps so many people through such difficult times.

Each year, 100,000 people are diagnosed with one of the three main types of cancer: breast, bowel and male lung cancer. But thanks to Cancer Research, mortality rates are at their lowest for 40 years. Cancer research attributes this to new and better treatments being made available.

The television adverts have real cancer patients in them. Cancer Research literally changes lives and lessens suffering...

Carol Sulton

> **Examiner's comment**
>
> The candidate has started her answer extremely well. Ideas are well presented and persuade the reader into wanting to donate to Cancer Research. Emotive language is used effectively. Paragraphs enhance meaning. This is the beginnings of an A-grade response.

Assessment for Learning

Complete the third paragraph, using another three rhetorical devices in your writing. Ask a partner to identify which three you have used. They should be clear.

Task G

Imagine that your favourite sporting hero passes away in a tragic accident. The unexpected news has come as a great shock. As a member of your hero/heroine's fan club, and a loyal and dedicated fan, you have been asked to write a speech on behalf of the fans. You will be making your speech in public.

Taking into account all that you have learned about rhetorical devices and from Earl Spencer's funeral oration, write a speech that is a suitable tribute to your sporting hero/heroine and his/her great qualities and achievements.

You might find it helpful to include some of the following phrases in your speech.

Opening phrases:
I stand before you today…
We have come to pay our last respects to…
We all feel the loss of…

Other phrases:
Only now you are gone do we…
The last time I saw…
We all remember…
He/she would want us to…
The way I will think of .... is as…

Closing phrases:
I would like to end by…
Above all…
I am proud to…

Student response to Task G

We have come to pay our last respects to .... I really liked .... He was my sporting hero. I feel he has done so much to inspire young people and encourage them to have an ambition in life. We, his fans, all feel his loss today.

Only now that .... has gone, do we realise the full impact he has made on the sporting world. He has set three world records for the…

Examiner's comment

This student has made a good C-grade start to this task. There is a clear structure and rhetorical devices are used. Paragraphs are well structured and varied. The candidate needs to sustain this level of response to achieve a C.

Assessment for Learning

Continue and complete the student response above, referring to a sporting hero of your choice. Try to use a minimum of one or two rhetorical devices in each paragraph. Identify and label which ones you have used in the margin.

You could even record your speech on tape or CD and listen to it to see how good you sound. Do you find what you say interesting?

And finally...

Shakespeare used rhetorical devices in his works. He used puns/plays on words very cleverly. In his play *Hamlet*, for example, he famously wrote 'to be or not to be, that is the question'. But you do not need to be famous to use rhetorical devices. Good awareness of writing techniques and practice will help you to become skilled in your own right.

Writing to inform, explain and describe

These three styles of writing are often linked. In order to do one there is normally some degree of reliance on one or both of the other two styles, although writing to describe can sometimes stand alone as this need not always be 100% factually accurate.

When we inform somebody about something, he or she may ask for an explanation, which may include some description. For example:

Inform   Student tells teacher she has not done her homework.

Explain   The teacher explains the importance and relevance of the set homework. This is still factual but has a little more detail.

Describe   The student then describes in more detail the circumstances which affected her being able to do the homework, e.g. 'I felt really sick and was in bed with a temperature for most of the night. I wish I had been able to finish my homework and I feel really awful but...'

Writing to inform and explain

Cyber Crime - Old Crimes, New Tools

The internet is an exciting and interesting tool, but the increase in on-line banking and shopping is being met by a rise in its use for criminal purposes.

Criminals carry out cyber crime from the comfort of their own home, office or internet café. They can work alone and commit crimes anywhere in the world.

However, there are ways to stop yourself being a victim. Simple crime prevention includes keeping anti-virus/firewall software up to date, anti-spyware programmes and thinking before replying to e-mails from unknown sources.

What are the con tricks and how do they work?

Phishing
A growing problem where offenders try to steal identity (usually bank details). First you receive an unsolicited e-mail, apparently from your bank. Thousands of these e-mails are sent in the knowledge that some will be received by someone who banks with the company they say they are from.

The genuine looking e-mail says they are reviewing accounts or have some problem that requires you to confirm your account details. They may provide a link to an on-screen form for you to complete which will be bogus and gives crooks your account details.

These will be used to empty your account. Banks, building societies or other finance bodies won't contact you for these details and e-mails like this should be treated with great suspicion. If you don't reply they can't get your details!

419 Scams
Sometimes referred to as Nigerian 419 scams, they often start with e-mail claiming to be from a bank employee, government official or relative of an important rich individual who has died.

The e-mail asks for your help to get a lot of money out of the country. In return you will receive a large part of this cash. If you respond they will ask for money for solicitors fees, administration costs and bank account details. People responding to this con have even been kidnapped when they went to collect their cash. This is a 'get-poor-quick' scheme.

Bogus Lottery Wins
The e-mail states you have won first prize in a lottery you haven't entered, in a foreign country you've never been to, certainly not recently, but you have won thousands of euros.

If you reply two things happen. You've confirmed their e-mail hit a correct address and they will then send a letter often containing a Trojan or Spyware virus. As soon as this is opened it infects your computer, giving access to your personal details.

Next you are asked for fees to receive your winnings. Any cheque will be stolen or counterfeit, you will cash it and as part of the agreement send some to the person who arranged your winnings. When the cheque is found to be false the money you sent will have disappeared, you will be responsible and a lot worse off.

eBay
The UK's largest on-line marketplace and e-commerce site, the World's Online Marketplace™ has a global customer base of 135m selling goods and services by a passionate community of individuals and small businesses.

The site has a global presence in 32 international markets. At any time over 44m items are for sale world wide, with 4m new items added each day. Founded in the UK in October 1999, eBay.co.uk has 10m users and over 3m items for sale daily.

Why is eBay safe?
The vast majority of buyers and sellers on eBay are honest and reliable. Millions of transactions take place every day without a problem, making it one of the safest places to trade on the web.

However you should follow trading guidelines and use common sense. Nearly all problems reported to police are where eBay members went outside the guidelines and ended up as victims of fraud or deception. There are bargains but don't be greedy - if it looks too good to be true it probably is.

If you sell, don't fall victim to phishing e-mails claiming to be from eBay or Paypal. Criminals want account details so they can steal your trading history and good name. The safety centre on eBay provides a wealth of information on how to trade safely on eBay, also what to do in the rare event that something goes wrong.

Commonly associated with e-trading are **escrow** sites. Escrow offers buyers and sellers peace of mind. It takes the risk out of letting buyers inspect items before final payment.
A successful escrow process works this way:
1. the buyer sends payment to the escrow company, a trusted third party
2. the seller ships the item to the buyer
3. the buyer inspects and approves the item
4. funds are paid to the seller.

Ensure you use a genuine escrow site - scams often involve sending money to a bogus site or them falsely claiming funds have been deposited.

Scam escrow sites may say they hold several thousand dollars/Euros as surety from the person you are dealing with. As you can see from the above example, that is not how these sites work.

Overpaying/cashback - you advertise goods for sale and are e-mailed by a 'buyer' who claims to live abroad. You're asked to accept a UK banker's draft for more than the goods' asking price. This offer will claim to come from a third UK party who owes money to the 'buyer' and asks you to send the difference as a money transfer to a 'shipping agent' once funds have cleared.

This is most likely attempted **fraud** with you as the intended victim. You receive a stolen cheque or draft that can be recalled by the bank even after funds have cleared and show on your account. Any money transferred by you cannot be recalled once sent and you lose your money.

Job offer scam - a spam e-mail arrives offering a job working from home for a few hours a week with big rewards. This is a bogus foreign company that wants to clear funds for goods sold in your country. Their clients pay money into your account and you send the money onto them by Western Union Money Transfer and you get a fee.

This is money laundering - money transferred to your account will be a result of criminal activity. When you send a cash transfer to an untraceable recipient, you could face a police investigation, as the paper trail will end at your account.

Surfing Safety
The internet is a great service when used properly, with a wealth of information, services, bargains and entertainment on-line. The following tips will keep you safe.

Safe Surfing Tips
- keep virus/firewall software up to date
- install anti-spyware
- keep your operating system up to date
- think before replying to unsolicited e-mail
- never send your account details to anyone
- never pay for goods using Western Union unless you know who you are sending the money to (this is also Western Union's advice).

Some Useful Web Sites

Further information can be found at:

www.ceop.gov.uk   (Child Exploitation and Online Protection Centre)

www.iwf.org.uk   (Internet Watch Foundation)

www.identitytheft.org.uk   (Home Office site)

www.ifccfbi.gov   (FBI site)

www.escrowfraud.com   (list of fake sites and advice)

www.crime-research.org   (voluntary-funded research group)

'Looking to the future the equation is simple, money is going electronic and where money goes so will organised crime'

Bill Hughes
(Director General National Crime Squad)

Escrow The process of an agent providing safe keeping of cash, securities and documents and handling the paperwork and transfer of funds for the borrower and seller.

*If you know anything about computer crime and want to remain anonymous contact the independent charity Crimestoppers on **0800 555 111** or via **www. crimestoppers-uk.org**

CRIMESTOPPERS
Staffordshire
0800 555 111
Call anonymously with information about crime

Task A

1 Read the Crimestoppers leaflet informing us about the dangers on the internet. Identify the purpose of the leaflet.

2 Copy and complete the table below, ticking as many of the features of a leaflet as you can identify in the Crimestoppers one. Refer back to Chapter 4 on writing formats (page 65) to refresh your memory of the key features of a leaflet, e.g. headings, sub-headings, bullet points, text boxes.

Feature	Tick	Feature	Tick	Feature	Tick
Headings		Use of pronouns, we, you, us etc.		Colloquial language	
Sub-headings		Illustrations		Graphs	
Bullet points		Web pages		Statistics	
Text boxes		E-mail addresses		Quotations from experts	
Statistics		Anecdotes		Humour	
Rhetorical questions		Irony		Numbered points	
Contact numbers		Emotive language		Other	
Addresses		Formal language			

Task B

Using the features you have identified in Task A, create your own leaflet on one of the following:
- Write and create a leaflet informing students about the dangers of the internet in schools. Explain to them what they need to look out for and how to keep the school rules regarding the use of the internet.
- Write and create a leaflet informing students about road safety and explaining how they can be safer on the roads.

Assessment for Learning

Highlight and label each feature in your own leaflet. Pick three features and explain their impact and effect on your intended audience.

Writing to describe

We can also use writing to describe something factual. When you are writing to describe, your main aim is to create a picture with words so that your audience can imagine vividly the place, scene, person, situation etc. Your choice of words is extremely important.

The sunset

Corel

Student 2

The orange orb lit up the bright resplendent[1] sky. I was transfixed; lost for a brief moment in the beauty of the scene, like a polar bear in the midst of the northern lights. Myriads[2] of razor-sharp rays cut through the sky, transforming the shoreline. I rubbed my hand along the rough edges of the balustrade[3] at the end of the pier and I winced as a splinter of wood caught my finger. The amber glow…

Student 1

The bright sun was in the blue sky. I stood and looked at it. I had seen it before. It was orange. I was feeling happy and cheerful. The sky was full of orange. I watched the sunset…

1 brilliant, glittering
2 vast numbers
3 railing supported by series of short pillars

Task A

1 Study the openings above from two students' descriptions of a sunset. You need to decide:

- Which one is more effective and why.
- How effective is student 1's description?
- How effective is student 2's description?

Highlight the interesting words in both extracts.

2 Read the examiner's comments below and try to remember what makes a better answer. You will apply your skills in writing a piece of your own in the next task.

Examiner's comment
Student 1

The student has thought about using description and is starting to build up images in the reader's mind. The sentences are effective but rather short. This piece of work would be awarded a Grade D in the exam. It could be improved by crafting longer sentences, using punctuation effectively and by using more descriptive language such as similes, alliteration and powerful adjectives.

Assessment for Learning

Redraft student 1's description using the advice given by the examiner above. Try to aim for a minimum of a Grade C answer. Refer back to the general grade criteria for writing table in Chapter 4 (page 61) to remind yourself of what needs to be included in a C-grade response.

Note: If your target grade is higher, refer back to the same table but try to plan, construct and write your answer to match the A-grade criteria.

Examiner's comment
Student 2

This student has made far better use of descriptive language. Linguistic devices are used effectively. Ideas are detailed and developed. The description is convincing and compelling and engages the reader fully. It is a Grade A response.

Assessment for Learning

1 Continue student 2's description, trying to remain focused on the examiner's comments. Try to continue as if you were the student writing the original response in the exam.
2 Check your work and mark it by highlighting and ticking where you meet the criteria for an A grade. Refer back to the general grade criteria for writing table in Chapter 4 (page 61) to remind yourself of what needs to be included in an A-grade response.

Task B

Using all the skills you have learned from the previous tasks, complete the task below.

You are on a bus which has stopped because of roadworks. Describe what you see and hear as you wait for the bus to move on.

Image DJ/Cadmium

Assessment for Learning

Check your work and self-assess which grade you are currently working at using the general grade criteria for writing table in Chapter 4 (page 61). Redraft your response, improving it, so you meet all or most of the criteria in the next grade above.

Remember: refer to mark schemes and Assessment Objectives when you are writing so that you get into the habit of knowing what is expected of you by your teacher and the examiner.

And finally...

Writing can be an exciting process and it is your responsibility to improve your work through dedication, practice, drafting and redrafting in response to assessment. All good writers plan their work. Many redraft work where possible or appropriate. Our work can always be improved and we can always learn more. With hard work and determination everyone can achieve success and become an even better writer, including you!

C

Speaking and listening

Chapter 6

Assessment Objectives for speaking and listening

Why does speaking and listening amount to 20% of the marks for GCSE English? The answer is found in what examiners need to assess.

Under the topic of speaking and listening, you are required to show that you can speak clearly in a range of activities to different audiences. You need to select appropriate vocabulary and be able to work with other people as well as on your own. Usually, your ability to communicate will be assessed orally, but your study of spoken language will be assessed in writing. To be successful, you must learn how the forms of speaking and listening differ and how they will be assessed.

For Unit 2 of the GCSE English and English Language courses you are required to complete three different types of controlled assessments: presenting; discussing and listening; and role playing. Each activity is marked separately out of 15 marks; the three marks are added together to give a final mark out of 45.

For GCSE English, your speaking and listening will be assessed against AO1. For GCSE English Language your speaking and listening will be assessed against both AO1 and AO2. These Assessment Objectives (AOs) are detailed below.

English/English Language: AO1 speaking and listening	
AO1(i)	• Speak to communicate clearly and purposefully; structure and sustain talk, adapting it to different situations and audiences; use Standard English and a variety of techniques as appropriate.
AO1(ii)	• Listen and respond to speakers' ideas and perspectives, and how they construct and express meanings.
AO1(iii)	• Interact with others, shaping meanings through suggestions, comments and questions and drawing ideas together.
AO1(iv)	• Create and sustain different roles.
English Language: AO2 study of spoken language	
AO2(i)	• Understand variations in spoken language, explaining why language changes in relation to contexts.
AO2(ii)	• Evaluate the impact of spoken language choices in their own and others' use.

This chapter looks at what is required to succeed at AO1. AO2 is covered in the next chapter.

AO1(i)

Speak to communicate clearly and purposefully; structure and sustain talk, adapting it to different situations and audiences; use Standard English and a variety of techniques as appropriate

Key words	What the key words mean
communicate clearly and purposefully	You talk to an audience and explain how you think and feel about something.
structure and sustain	You organise your material into a logical order and speak at length about it.
adapting it	You change your language to fit the age and membership of your audience: a talk to a group of five-year-old children would have different language and presentation to one to your headteacher.
use Standard English	You use the kind of language you would be expected to use in written tests.

Where is AO1(i) assessed?

This AO is assessed just about everywhere you are being assessed for speaking and listening: it is the fundamental test of whether you can communicate. In English and English Language all speaking and listening AOs are examined in Unit 2.

How is AO1(i) assessed?

Your teacher will give you a controlled assessment at some time during your course. Your work will be marked by your teacher and moderated by the examination board.

Grade A	A personal response which covers the topic in detail and includes sophisticated vocabulary while using Standard English appropriately.
Grade C	A personal response which communicates information and points of view, including a range of vocabulary and sentence structures while using Standard English competently.
Grade F	A short response which gives some points of view and ideas, including straightforward vocabulary while using some Standard English.

This Assessment Objective is all about speaking. In order to gain a Grade C or above you need to think about what it means in practice:

- You must understand the basic content: you must know what you are talking about and have plenty to tell your audience.
- You must be able to explain not just what you think and feel but also why.
- You must keep the interest of your audience by using different techniques, such as having long and short sentences, using rhetorical questions or including exciting or humorous sections.

> **Remember:** when you are speaking, you must decide what the audience needs to know, what evidence you can supply to back up your views and how to make it interesting.

Task A

Read the article 'School uniform stinks' on the following page. Give a talk to the rest of the class explaining what you think about school uniform and the changes you would like to see made to it.

Note: Tasks B–D will help you complete this task in a structured way.

Student response to Task A

I think that school uniform should be abolished. I don't like wearing it and none of my mates do either. It is designed by people who don't have to wear it. I think my uniform makes me look stupid and I wouldn't wear it if I didn't have to. I think a better uniform would be to have a polo shirt and not a tie. I think we should be able to wear shorts in the summer because we would be more comfortable.

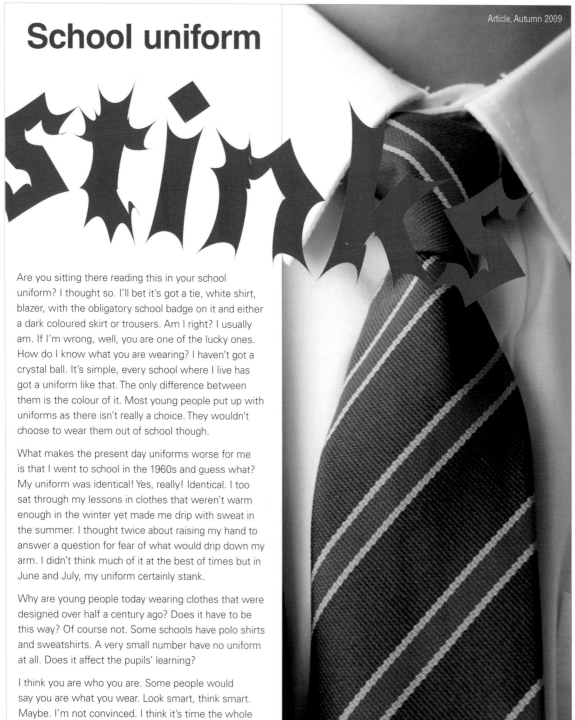

School uniform stinks

Article, Autumn 2009

Are you sitting there reading this in your school uniform? I thought so. I'll bet it's got a tie, white shirt, blazer, with the obligatory school badge on it and either a dark coloured skirt or trousers. Am I right? I usually am. If I'm wrong, well, you are one of the lucky ones. How do I know what you are wearing? I haven't got a crystal ball. It's simple, every school where I live has got a uniform like that. The only difference between them is the colour of it. Most young people put up with uniforms as there isn't really a choice. They wouldn't choose to wear them out of school though.

What makes the present day uniforms worse for me is that I went to school in the 1960s and guess what? My uniform was identical! Yes, really! Identical. I too sat through my lessons in clothes that weren't warm enough in the winter yet made me drip with sweat in the summer. I thought twice about raising my hand to answer a question for fear of what would drip down my arm. I didn't think much of it at the best of times but in June and July, my uniform certainly stank.

Why are young people today wearing clothes that were designed over half a century ago? Does it have to be this way? Of course not. Some schools have polo shirts and sweatshirts. A very small number have no uniform at all. Does it affect the pupils' learning?

I think you are who you are. Some people would say you are what you wear. Look smart, think smart. Maybe. I'm not convinced. I think it's time the whole uniform issue was opened up to wider debate.

Woodsy/Fotolia

6

Examiner's comment

The speaker makes a series of points but none of them are expanded. The main ideas are expressed clearly, generally using Standard English. There are some attempts to explain the speaker's thinking and feelings. This answer would fulfil the Grade F descriptors.

How to improve

The candidate needs to expand on the ideas by giving more details and explaining his/her reasons more fully.

Assessment for Learning

Identify two things which this student has done well and two things that could have been better. Discuss your findings with a partner.

Task B

1 Copy and complete the grid below to outline the content of a talk on school uniform that will get you at least a Grade C. Then share your grid with a partner. Compare what you both have written and add any new ideas to your own grid.

Good things about school uniform	Why do you think this?
1	
2	
3	
4	
5	

2 Copy and add to the grid below to show what changes you would make to your uniform.

What changes would you make?	Reasons
Shirt?	1 2
Tie?	1 2

3 Now write a paragraph of a talk you will give to the rest of your class about your thoughts on uniform.

Exchange your paragraph with another student and assess whether you think it explains what he or she thinks and why. Decide whether it would keep the audience's interest. Now write notes on it to explain to your partner how to improve it.

How can you improve your grade?

To gain a Grade C or above, you have to explain clearly what you think and why. To improve on it you need to be able to make your thoughts come alive for the audience. This means they have to feel what you feel. Try to include stories about yourself or perhaps others in the class to keep the audience interested. Involve your listeners by using rhetorical questions. Look back at the article, 'School Uniform Stinks', and try to identify how the writer has spoken directly to the audience.

Pressmaster/Fotolia

Task C

Complete the main part of your speech on school uniform by including all the changes you want to make with reasons for them.

Task D

Write an opening and an ending to your speech that will grab the audience's interest and leave them wanting more.

> **Remember:** there are three parts to this activity: the opening; your ideas and explanations; and the ending. They are all important.

Student response to Task D

Opening

Are you sitting comfortably? Probably not and it's not just the chairs either! At this moment I'm itching, literally, to get this uniform off and get into something less scratchy and more relaxed. I don't know about you, but whenever I put this uniform on, I don't feel like a real person any more. I feel like a cog, meshed up in a giant machine along with hundreds of other identical cogs. Let's face it, I might like you, but that doesn't mean I want to be like you. What I mean is, I'm me and you're you. We don't think the same. Why should we look the same?

Ending

Uniform? That's it! That's the problem. We aren't uniform so why are our clothes? We've all got different backgrounds and want different things for our futures. Look around you. We are all individuals. We come in all different shapes and colours. Uniform shouldn't mean 'one size fits all'.

Examiner's comment

This candidate uses a range of techniques to draw the audience into the speech and to maintain interest. There is confident use of the word 'you' in both the opening and the ending. This makes the listener feel part of the talk. There is clever use of a variety of sentence lengths, for instance at the start of the final section. This is an individual response and the character of the speaker comes across clearly. It is a persuasive response that appears spontaneous but is sophisticated in its use of grammar and the way it communicates complex ideas. The theme of uniform and uniformity is sustained throughout the talk and is used as the main vehicle to highlight the speaker's priorities, views and perspectives. The candidate shows an assured use of Standard English vocabulary and grammar but is prepared to depart from this deliberately in order to make a point.

This candidate's work is worthy of a Grade A.

How to improve

The candidate needs to use more sophisticated vocabulary and to include the audience in the final paragraph.

AO1(ii)

Listen and respond to speakers' ideas, perspectives and how they construct and express their meanings

Key words	What the key words mean
respond to speakers' ideas	You listen to what other people say and make comments on it or question it.
perspectives	You understand what people are trying to say and ask questions to make sure.
how they construct and express meanings	You look for examples of bias or prejudice in what people say.

Where is AO1(ii) assessed?

This AO is all about working with other people, discussing ideas and coming to conclusions. It can be assessed wherever you are involved in group or pair work that involves you giving your opinions or working towards a presentation. In English and English Language all speaking and listening AOs are examined in Unit 2.

How is AO1(ii) assessed?

Your teacher will give you a controlled assessment at some time during your course. Your work will be marked by your teacher and moderated by the examination board. Although you will be working with other people, you will receive an individual mark which might not be the same as the mark given to the other people you work with.

Grade A	You manage your group/pair by listening carefully and asking questions to find out exactly what is meant while also putting forward your own thoughts and encouraging other people to take part in order to complete the task fully and on time.
Grade C	You listen closely, ask questions and put forward your own ideas while questioning bias or prejudice in other people's thoughts.
Grade F	You put forward your own ideas. You show some interest in what other people are saying and you sometimes add your own thoughts while allowing other people to express their ideas.

This Assessment Objective is about both speaking and listening. In order to gain a Grade C or above you need to think about what it means in practice:

- You must put forward your ideas.
- You must listen carefully to what other people say and respond to it.
- You must be able to explain not just what you think and feel but also why.
- You must show that you understand what is being said by other people.
- You must ask questions to encourage other people to explain fully.

Remember: when you are speaking, you must explain fully but give other people the chance to speak. When you are listening, show your understanding through your body language and your spoken responses.

Task A

1 Look at the four pictures of different types of holiday. Copy and complete the grid below to rank order them from 1 to 4, where '1' is the holiday you would most like and '4' is the holiday you would least like. Use the final column to explain your reasons. Do not just put that you would enjoy it or that it would be boring. Explain why.

	Rank order	*Reason*
Tropical beach		
Skiing		
Canal barge		
New York		

2 Now share your thoughts with other people in a small group. Ask questions to find out what the others think. Use the grid to help you structure your conversation. Try to reach an agreement on which holiday you think is best and give reasons for your choice.

Task B

In the same group, discuss what you think is the best possible holiday. You do not have to come to an agreement, but you do need to explain your thoughts and listen to those of other people.

Student response to Task B

Right I'll start then. My best place for me to go on holiday has got to be Benidorm. For starters, everyone speaks English. You never have to worry about foreign food because you can get all day English breakfasts. The sun shines every day. It's really hot so you get a great tan but you have to be careful not to look like a lobster. You can have a right laugh with your mates in the hotel pool and at night you just party till morning. Sangria's dead cheap. It's easy to get to and it doesn't take long to fly there. That's me finished. I don't care what you lot think.

Examiner's comment

The speaker makes a series of points but none of them is expanded. The main ideas are clearly expressed, generally using Standard English but there are some examples of non-Standard English. There are some attempts to explain the speaker's thinking and feelings but it feels like a slightly expanded list. The speaker does not attempt to involve anyone else in the discussion and does not display any listening skills. This would fulfil some of the Grade F descriptors.

How to improve

The candidate needs to listen and respond to the other people in the group, not just tell them what he/she thinks.

Identify one thing which this student has done well and two things that could have been better. Discuss your findings with a partner.

> **Remember:**
> there are two parts to this activity: speaking and listening. What you decide is not important. How you reach the decision is vital.

Task C

Discuss with a partner or in a small group which places are good for holidays and what you could do if you went there. Before you start, copy and complete the grid below to help structure your thoughts.

Where would you want to go?	
Things you would want to do there	**Reasons**
Reasons why your holiday destination is the best possible one	

Start your discussions and talk to each other for two minutes. Then stop and tell the other group members what they have done well and how they can improve. Start the discussion again and try to include all the advice you have just been given.

Student response to Task C

Joanna: We went to Benidorm last year. Have you ever been there?

Lesley: No we've only ever been to Spain a couple of times: once to the north and once to the south to a small town near Nerja.

Joanna: We've been to Nerja. My uncle used to own a holiday home there. Can you believe we once saw dolphins swimming just off the beach?

Lesley: That must have been brilliant. Was it much like Benidorm?

Joanna: A bit, but Benidorm has more high-rise flats and British visitors. Some people call it Beniyork because of its skyline. It's also got an old town but it's dwarfed by the newer buildings. In the summer the population is ten times greater than in the winter. That means it's really lively at night.

Lesley: I don't think I'd like that very much. We went to Austria last year. I felt like I was in *The Sound of Music* when we visited Saltzburg. The city was quite compact, almost antiquated, but that wasn't the only thing that impressed me. I was inspired by the panoramic views of the Alps and

Bebow/Fotolia

LoopAll/Fotolia

the charm of the picturesque villages. I don't like it when it's really hot. What about you? Would you ever consider not going on a beach holiday?

Examiner's comment

Although this is only the opening of the discussion, both candidates are expressing their opinions. Each of them draws the other into the conversation by asking questions which are also used to clarify meanings and get further information. Neither candidate is ignoring the other one and both are exploring the topic. Lesley is beginning to expand on her ideas but Joanna has not fully expressed hers yet. The main ideas are clearly expressed using Standard English. Both speakers explain their thinking but Lesley uses more sophisticated language and sentence structures. If the discussion continued at this level Joanna would fulfil all the Grade C descriptors while Lesley would be moving towards a Grade A.

How to improve

Joanna needs to develop her ideas by explaining them in more detail. Lesley should encourage Joanna to justify her thoughts more and challenge any evidence of bias in Joanna's thoughts.

How can you improve your grade?

You should ask yourself the following questions while taking part in discussions:

- Am I expressing myself clearly? Do other people know what I mean?
- Is everyone involved? How can I make sure everyone has their say?
- Have I asked enough questions of the other people?
- Am I using sophisticated or simple vocabulary?

AO1(iii)

Interact with others, shaping meaning through suggestions, comments and questions and drawing ideas together

Key words	What the key words mean
interact	You take a full part in the activity and work with other people by listening to what they say and making comments on it or questioning it.
shaping meanings	You work through ideas together to develop them and express them in ways that you can all understand.
drawing ideas together	At the end of the task you go over all of the ideas to enable you to come to a conclusion.

Where is AO1(iii) assessed?

This AO is also about working with other people, discussing ideas and coming to conclusions. It can be assessed wherever you are involved in group or pair work that involves you giving your opinions or working towards a presentation. In English and English Language all speaking and listening AOs are examined in Unit 2.

How is AO1(iii) assessed?

Your teacher will give you a controlled assessment. This could take place at any time during your course. Your work will be marked by your teacher and moderated by the examination board. Although you will be working with other people, you will receive an individual mark which might not be the same as the mark the other people you work with get.

Grade A	You manage your group/pair by listening carefully and asking questions to find out exactly what is meant while also putting forward your own thoughts and encouraging other people to take part in order to complete the task fully and on time.
Grade C	You listen closely, ask questions and put forward your own ideas while questioning bias or prejudice in other people's thoughts. You make significant contributions to the discussion.
Grade F	You put forward your own ideas. You show some interest in what other people are saying and you sometimes add your own thoughts while allowing other people to express their ideas.

This Assessment Objective is about both speaking and listening. In order to gain a Grade C or above you need to think about what it means in practice:

- You must put forward your ideas.
- You must listen carefully to what other people say and respond to it.
- You must be able to explain not just what you think and feel but also why.
- You must show that you understand what is being said by other people.
- You must ask questions to encourage other people to explain fully.

Task A

Read the 'Teach the teacher' article on texting. In a pair or small group, plan a presentation that you will give to the rest of the class. It should be on something that you know a lot about.

Note: Your presentation does not have to be on texting but this example will focus on that. You may not actually have to give the presentation as you could be marked on your contribution to the discussion (including listening) that is needed to plan the presentation.

1 Start by creating a list of all of the text abbreviations you know. Share these with your partner. Make up a title for your presentation and write it in text.

2 Now, individually, make notes on:
- why people use texting
- how to text: the best techniques
- when and what to text
- text shortcuts
- what you think of texting

Remember: there are two parts to this activity: speaking and listening. *What* you decide is not important. *How* you reach the decision is vital. You must discuss the plan.

3 Share your notes with your partner. You must now decide what to include in your presentation. You should decide first on the order and then on the content of each section. You might want to do this as a flow chart.

Introduction (Iqbal)
What texting is and how it developed

⬇

How to text (Ahmed)
Using the thumb

⬇

What to text (Iqbal)

4 Decide who will say each part and how it will be said. You are allowed to use visual aids and presentational software such as PowerPoint to support your presentation so you should discuss how you would use them in your planning.

TEACH THE TEACHER

Teachers are clever, aren't they? Of course they are. You might as well admit it, even if you don't want to. They have to be clever or they wouldn't be teaching. But how clever are they? Can you do anything better than your teachers? You might do free running. How many teachers can do that? Come to that, how many of you can? You might be the next big singing sensation. How long will you last? You might be able to read minds, handy when you're having a test. Teachers would love to be able to do that. Some of them think they can: 'Don't lie to me. I know what you're thinking.' If they did, you'd be in real trouble!

No, it's more likely that you think you can't do anything better than your teachers because they're clever. Remember? Well, now's your chance to make your mark. You'll need a little help. It's in your pocket or your bag. It's your mobile phone. Don't get it out now! You can do something with that little phone that teachers would just kill to be able to do.

You can text.

Wouldn't they like to be able to do that? Wouldn't they love to know what all the little words mean? LOL!!!!
So, ru ok 4 sum fun 2day?

Monkey Business/Fotolia

Student response to Task A

Iqbal: What are we going to say about how to text?

Ahmed: I don't think we should just say it. I think it would be better to show it because that way the audience would be able to see what we were doing.

Iqbal: That's a good idea. We could take it in turns to demonstrate. You could text using your thumb and I could show them using my finger. I'm much quicker using my thumbs. We could do with a way of showing that it's the best way to do it. Any ideas?

Ahmed: We could have a race! We could ask someone to give us a message to text then we could both do it and see which of us finished first. That would prove it.

Iqbal: What if people thought we were cheating?

Ahmed: It doesn't matter. We're only giving our opinions. If they don't agree, it's up to them.

Iqbal: Will they be able to see well enough? I've watched loads of presentations where they show things and you can't see them because they're not big enough.

Ahmed: I've just had a great idea! We could make a video.

Iqbal: But we're doing a talk, aren't we?

Ahmed: Exactly! We make a video of one of us texting. We focus in close on the phone and the thumb so they can see what we're doing. Then we import it into PowerPoint or Moviemaker and we show it while we talk over it to explain it.

Iqbal: I like that. So, let's make sure we've got it all sorted. What are we going to have in this section?

Examiner's comment

Both of the candidates take a full part in the discussion, but Ahmed has more ideas. Iqbal looks to Ahmed to lead the discussion by asking him questions. He also uses these questions to clarify the meaning of what Ahmed is saying. He encourages Ahmed and begins to take control with the last statement which draws them back to the structure of their presentation. Ahmed is more animated, but he explains clearly what he thinks should happen. He does not really give Iqbal the opportunity to contribute many ideas. Both students make significant contributions that move the discussion on. They both listen and respond to each other, engaging with their ideas and feelings. If the discussion continued in a similar way, both students would fulfil the criteria for a Grade C.

How to improve

Iqbal needs to contribute more ideas and explain more. Ahmed should let Iqbal into the conversation more and encourage him to explain his thoughts.

Assessment for Learning

When you are rehearsing, ask the other members of your group to grade your performance. Get them to tell you if you are doing enough and how realistic it seems to them. Discuss with your group which ideas work and what needs to be done to make them more realistic.

How can you improve your grade?

You should ask yourself the following questions while taking part in a discussion:

- Am I putting forward my ideas clearly? Do I need to explain more?
- Am I showing that I am listening by responding to what is being said?
- Have I said enough?
- Have I asked enough questions to let my partner explain fully?

> **Remember:** make sure you contribute enough to score highly. When you are speaking, you must explain fully but give other people a chance to speak. When you are listening, show your understanding through your body language and your spoken responses.

AO1(iv)

Create and sustain different roles

Key words	What the key words mean
create	You make up new characters or adapt existing ones.
sustain roles	You stay in character throughout an extended performance.

Where is AO1(iv) assessed?

This AO is about performing a piece of drama. It can be assessed when you are working with other people or it could be a presentation on your own. It must be improvised. In English and English Language all speaking and listening AOs are examined in Unit 2.

How is AO1(iv) assessed?

Your teacher will give you a controlled assessment in which you will need to take on the role of a character and perform as that character. This could take place at any time during your course. Your work will be marked by your teacher and moderated by the examination board. Although you will be working with other people, you will receive an individual mark which might not be the same as the marks the other people you work with get.

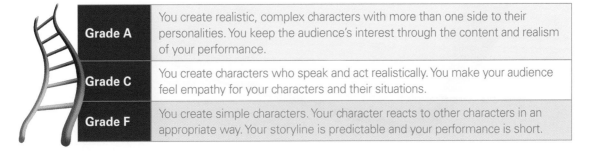

Grade A	You create realistic, complex characters with more than one side to their personalities. You keep the audience's interest through the content and realism of your performance.
Grade C	You create characters who speak and act realistically. You make your audience feel empathy for your characters and their situations.
Grade F	You create simple characters. Your character reacts to other characters in an appropriate way. Your storyline is predictable and your performance is short.

Speaking and listening

This Assessment Objective is about performing. In order to gain a Grade C or above you need to think about what it means in practice:

- You must take on a significant role.
- You must work with other people to create a realistic situation.
- You must be able to make your audience believe in your character.
- You must show a range of gestures and movements.
- You must use your voice to express how you are feeling.

Remember: when you are performing, you must stay in role as the character you are playing.

Missing

Chapter 1

The clock slowly struggled round until the hands read six o'clock. James Dawson waited with growing impatience. His daughter, Claire, should have been home over an hour ago. He could not understand what had happened. She was usually such a punctual girl that he had begun to worry about her safety. Despite all of his efforts to control his imagination, James found himself fearing the worst. Why hadn't she telephoned? Where could she be?

Two hours ago Claire had left to visit her friend, Jenny, who lived on the other side of the park. James tried desperately to repel the thoughts that were invading his brain. Finally he could not withstand the pressure any more. All his senses told him something was wrong. In the whirlpool of his mind, James' emotions swirled together and from within the turmoil he could hear Claire's voice shouting, 'Call the police!'

The sound of his daughter's voice brought James back to reality. His fingers, suddenly large and ungainly, fumbled as he tried to ring the emergency number. With panic flowing through his veins like a swollen river, he stumbled wildly through the three digits. He heard the comforting voice say, 'Emergency. Which service do you require?'

As James Dawson told his tale to the police officer, he heard the quiet click of the front door opening…

Laurent Renault/Fotolia

School Report

Chapter 1

My mother was sitting in her favourite chair. As usual, the cat was curled up in its prime position on her knee, facing the fire. I had sat outside the door for over twenty minutes wondering how to explain away the contents of my report. It was going to be difficult this time, even for someone with as much practice as I had.

I had thought of pretending that we had a new system this year, an online one that had crashed and all of the reports had been lost, but I didn't think that would work for long. She would only ring the school up to complain. I decided I would have to be more devious than that. What I needed was to get my mother in a good mood first, then she might be more receptive to the disaster I was carrying in my bag. Suddenly I knew what I would do. First, I would make a cup of tea and accompany it with one of my mother's favourite chocolate biscuits.

It would have been nice to get the chance to try my ploy out. As I entered the cosy room, the warmth disguised the frosty reception I was about to receive. My mother's face twisted into a half sneer as she held out a hand in my direction. The game was up! Handling my report with the delicacy one would use on a hand-grenade, I passed it to my mother and stood back, waiting for the inevitable explosion…

Anna Sushkova/Fotolia

Fury

Chapter 1

There was very little in Laura's life which annoyed her quite as much as her sister, Nicole. Ever since Laura could remember, she had never agreed with her sister. There was nothing unusual in that, everyone Laura knew hated their little sisters. This was different though. Nicole had gone to her friend's party wearing Laura's new top. Again, there was nothing unusual about that either. Nicole frequently 'borrowed' her sister's clothes without permission.

The unusual thing was that this time the top had reappeared in the wardrobe. This was quite staggering. Usually Laura had to threaten to burn all of Nicole's clothes to get her own returned. 'If only Nicole could be honest,' thought Laura as she pulled the top out.

Rage exploded inside Laura's head. Across the front of the garment, like a piece of modern art, was a huge red stain. The fury in Laura's eyes was matched by the colour and intensity of the mark. Without hesitating she raced downstairs to the living room where Nicole was talking to some of her friends. The door crashed open and Laura stared accusingly at her sister while waving the ruined top like a Roman standard bearer…

Task A

In pairs or a small group, prepare a performance for the rest of your class in which you explore the theme of family relationships.

1 Read the openings of the three novels: *Missing*, *School Report* and *Fury*.
2 Choose one of the openings from these novels and create a piece of drama based around it, using it as your starting point. You can change the characters to fit the people in your group. For instance, Mr Dawson could be Mrs Dawson. Copy and complete the grid below to help you plan your performance.

How will you begin?	Who will play the characters mentioned in the opening?	Do you need any other characters and who will play them?

Remember: you need to make sure that everyone has a large enough role to score well.

Plan out what will happen in your performance. You need to think about how each character will be identified. You also need to decide whether you want an open or closed ending. The grid below gives you an example of how to plan your work using *Fury* as a starting point. You could use a similar grid or you could choose a completely different format.

	Events
Opening	Laura enters the room where Nicole, Jake, Carla and Tom are listening to a CD. She turns the music off and demands to know what has happened to her top.
Continuation	Nicole denies all knowledge of the top or the mark. Her friends defend her, saying she didn't wear it to the party.
New idea or conflict	Laura leaves the room but returns with a top belonging to Nicole and a pair of scissors. She gives Nicole ten seconds to confess or she will start to cut the top up.
Continuation	Laura starts to count. Nicole's friends each try to persuade Laura to not cut up the top.
Ending/ resolution	When Laura reaches nine, the telephone rings. Nicole answers it. It is their mother. Nicole passes the telephone to Laura with the comment, 'It's Mum. She wants to tell you something about your top.'

Note: Writing a script is *not* allowed in the role-playing controlled assessment. This means you will have to improvise your performance. This does not mean that you cannot rehearse it though. For each of the events in your improvisation, you should make a list of the things you are going to say and how you are going to say them. You should think about your movements and gestures.

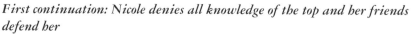

Assessment for Learning

Complete a planning grid by yourself then share your thoughts with the other members of your group. Discuss with your group which are the best ideas and what needs to be done to make them more realistic. As a group, complete a new grid, including all the ideas you have just had.

Student response to Task A

> **Remember:** you need to make your performance realistic so you should show a range of emotions.

First continuation: Nicole denies all knowledge of the top and her friends defend her

Nicole: Don't be ridiculous, Laura. Of course I haven't worn it. Why would I want to? It's minging. I wouldn't be seen dead in it. In fact, that's the only way I'd be seen in it. Tell her Tom.

Tom: It's true. Nicole never wore that top. I should know, I was looking at her enough!

Laura: Well, you would say that, wouldn't you? You're just trying to impress her. Well, don't think I can't see through your little game. She's got you wrapped round her little finger. You're just like a puppy dog, you do everything she says. Sit Tom. Heel Tom. Beg Tom.

Jake: That's not fair, Laura. All right, Tom might fancy Nicole but that doesn't stop him telling the truth. She wasn't even wearing a top. She was wearing a blue dress.

Laura: Hah! Caught you out! Nicole hasn't got a blue dress. How do you explain that then? Go on. I'd love to hear you talk your way out of that.

Nicole: It was your dress.

Laura: What?

Nicole: It was your dress.

Laura: My blue dress?

Carla: Yes, your blue dress, the one with the white collar. Nicole looked fantastic in it. Everybody was looking at her.

Tom: I certainly was.

Jake: So was I!

Carla: What?

Jake: Sorry.... But she did look good.

Laura: Right, that's it.

Nicole: Where are you going?

Laura: You'll see.

SemA/Fotolia

Examiner's comment

All the candidates take part in the improvisation but they do not perform equally. Laura and Nicole both have significant roles which they sustain and develop to move the drama on convincingly. There are plenty of opportunities for them to use a variety of verbal and non-verbal techniques. The other three characters are less well developed and are limited to minor, supporting roles.

Laura and Nicole would comfortably achieve a C grade, but the others would need to have much greater involvement in subsequent scenes if they are to approach that grade. At present they are more representative of F-grade candidates. This is partly the result of having so many people in the drama. The focus is on Nicole and Laura. If the scene continued after Laura's exit, there would be opportunities for them to talk about what they had just witnessed and how they felt about it. They would be able to express their opinions freely without Laura being present, but Nicole would need to give them the chance to do so with little interference as she would be likely to have another major role to play on Laura's return. The three friends would need to take larger roles themselves in subsequent scenes.

Assessment for Learning

Ask your partner to grade your performance. Get him or her to tell you if you are doing enough and what you need to do to improve.

How can you improve your grade?

You should ask yourself the following questions while taking part in an improvisation:

- Am I creating and sustaining my character? Does the audience believe in me?
- Is everyone involved? How can I make sure everyone has their say?
- Have I said enough?
- Am I using realistic vocabulary?
- Have I used any non-verbal forms of communication, e.g. pauses, meaningful looks, movements?

Remember: make sure you contribute enough to score highly.

Generic grade descriptions for speaking and listening

There are four parts to AO1 but you only have to do three controlled assessments. How can this be possible? Almost every speaking and listening task that you do will cover more than one part of AO1. The three tasks are broken down into:

- communicating and adapting language
- interacting and responding
- creating and sustaining roles

Each of these areas has its own specific grade descriptions, but there are also generic descriptions that summarise all the activities.

Grade A	You select suitable styles and registers of spoken English for a range of different situations and contexts. You use Standard English assuredly where appropriate. Your sentence structures will be varied, as will your vocabulary. You will give expert explanations. By initiating conversations and listening carefully, you will sustain contributions and develop group discussions. In both formal and creative settings, you fulfil the demands of different roles.
Grade C	You adapt your talk to different situations. You recognise where Standard English is required and use it confidently. You will use a range of sentence structures and vocabulary to communicate ideas clearly. Through careful listening and by developing ideas, you will make a significant contribution to discussions and creative activities.
Grade F	You talk confidently in familiar situations. You clearly convey your ideas and feelings. When you listen, it is with concentration and you make relevant responses. You attempt to meet the demands of different roles.

Most of speaking and listening is common sense. We speak and listen every day. The trick is to know how to do it in different situations. The most important thing to remember is your audience. You have to communicate clearly. That means not only being clear in what you say but also in how you say it. Think of the effect your facial expressions, gestures and body language will have on other people. Look them in the eye, believe in what you are saying and make everyone want to listen to you. Smile and be interesting and your audience will be all ears.

C

Speaking and listening

Chapter 7

Assessment: studying spoken language

If you are studying GCSE English Language you will be required to submit a language study assignment. This is worth 10% of your total GCSE marks and will be assessed according to AO2.

English Language: AO2 study of spoken language	
AO2(i)	• Understand variations in spoken language, explaining why language changes in relation to contexts.
AO2(ii)	• Evaluate the impact of spoken language choices in their own and others' use.

AO2(i)

Understand variations in spoken language, explaining why language changes in relation to contexts

Key words	What the key words mean
understand variations	You show that you know how spoken language is used for different outcomes.
explaining language changes	You can tell the examiner the reasons for the different uses of spoken English.
contexts	You understand how language changes to fit the age and membership of your audience. A discussion with your friends about how to plan a presentation to the rest of the class would have different language to the actual presentation itself.

Where is AO2(i) assessed?

This AO is assessed in GCSE English Language Unit 3: understanding spoken and written language and writing creatively. It is specifically covered in Unit 3 part c: studying spoken language. This is worth 10% of your final GCSE marks.

How is AO2(i) assessed?

Your teacher will give you a controlled assessment. This could take place at any time during your course. Your work will be marked by your teacher and moderated by the examination board. This assessment can only be done in writing.

This is a completely new assessment so it is worth spending some time getting to know and understand what you will have to do before we look at some tasks.

You will need to show that you understand how spoken language evolves in response to changes in society and technology and how this process relates to identity and cultural diversity.

This means you must:

- reflect critically on your own language use and that of other people in different contexts
- engage with real-life uses of talk, e.g. how language changes over time, Standard versus non-Standard English, regional variations in dialect and accents

This assessment should be based around an enquiry. This means that you will need to collect evidence or data and be able to analyse it and comment upon it. You can work in groups to do this but your final assessment must be an individual one.

Your assessment should be 800–1,000 words long.

Your teacher will set your task but it will cover the following three broad topic areas:

- social attitudes to spoken language
- spoken genres
- multi-modal talk

Topic	What this involves
Social attitudes to spoken language	This will give you opportunities to consider the ways in which: • certain types of speech are privileged in some societies and other types are less privileged • identity is established and conformity resisted through speech
Spoken genres	This will give you opportunities to study talk in various genres, including the media.
Multi-modal talk	This is a new idea which will let you study ways in which: • new technologies blur traditional distinctions between speaking and writing, providing new genres which have elements of both • online identity is established and negotiated • online talk is seen as potentially ambiguous

Grade A	A perceptive analysis of how you and other people use and adapt spoken English for different purposes using sophisticated interpretation, analysis and evaluations of your key data.
Grade C	A confident explanation of how you and others use and adapt spoken English for specific purposes including analysis of your data and of public attitudes to spoken language variations.
Grade F	A response which shows some awareness of how you and others use and adapt spoken language for specific purposes including some understanding of your data and some awareness of public attitudes to spoken language variations.

This Assessment Objective is all about investigating, analysing and explaining. In order to gain a Grade C or above you need to think about what it means in practice:

• You must conduct an investigation into language use: you must collect enough evidence for you to be able to analyse it.
• You must be able to explain your conclusions and support them with your evidence.
• You must be able to give your own opinions as well as stating what your investigation has found out.

You only do one assessment so your response will need to cover both AO2(i) and AO2(ii).

AO2(ii)

Evaluate the impact of spoken language choices in their own and others' use

Key words	What the key words mean
evaluate the impact	You analyse your evidence to show the effect of different types of spoken language.
spoken language choices	You can tell the examiner what choices of language are being made and explain the reasons for the different uses of spoken English.
own and others' use	You understand how language changes to fit the age and membership of your audience — a discussion with your friends about how to plan a presentation to the rest of the class would have different language to the actual presentation itself.

Where is AO2(ii) assessed?

This AO is assessed in the same unit as AO2(i) — GCSE English Language Unit 3: understanding spoken and written language and writing creatively. It is specifically covered in Unit 3 part c: studying spoken language.

How is AO2(ii) assessed?

This AO is assessed in the same controlled assessment as AO2(i).

This part of AO2 is all about analysing and explaining. In order to gain a Grade C or above you need to think about what it means in practice:

- You must analyse the information you have gathered.
- You must be able to explain your conclusions and support them with your evidence.
- You must be able to give your own opinions as well as stating what your investigation has found out.

That's quite a lot to take in so let's have a look at some tasks. There are three possible areas on which to answer so we'll look at tasks for each of them in turn.

Social attitudes to spoken language

Assessment task

Show how accents and dialects can influence our views of other people and how spoken language can establish our identities and sometimes resist conformity.

Remember: this is about analysis and explanation. You need to get some data or evidence first.

Before you begin this assessment task, you need to be clear about what accents and dialects are:

- **Accent:** this is the way the words are pronounced. It is how the speaker makes the words sound. For instance, someone from London would generally sound different to someone from Glasgow because of his or her accent.
- **Dialect:** this is the actual words that are being spoken. It describes the use of words in some parts of the country that are not used in other areas. For instance, an alley is known in some parts of the country as a passageway, an entry, a ginnel, a snicket or a tenfoot.

So where do we get our accents and dialects from? You could do some internet research on this.

It is not just whether you pronounce bath 'barth' or scone 'scon'. Both accents and dialects come from where we live. We learn to speak by copying the people around us. It is a bit like learning a foreign language. We get our accents by learning to pronounce words in the way those around us do. It is not deliberate, it just happens. If you move to another part of the country you will find your accent will change and become more like that of the people you hear speak each day.

Claudiaveja/Fotolia

Read the poem (opposite) from 'Unrelated Incidents' by Tom Leonard.

The poem is written phonetically: as it should be spoken. The spelling of the words reflects the Glaswegian accent of the speaker in the poem. If you put the poem through a spell-checker, what do you think would happen?

this is thi
six a clock
news thi
man said n
thi reason
a talk wia
BBC accent
iz coz yi
widny wahnt
mi ti talk
aboot thi
trooth wia
voice lik
wanna yoo
scruff. if
a toktaboot
thi trooth
lik wanna yoo
scruff yi
widny thingk
it wuz troo.
jist wonna yoo
scruff tokn.
thirza right
way ti spell
ana right way
to tok it. this
is me tokn yir
right way a
spellin. this
is ma trooth.
yooz doant no
thi trooth
yirseltz cawz
yi canny talk
right. this is
the six a clock
nyooz. belt
up.

Speaking and listening

In an interview in 2003, the author, Tom Leonard, said, 'I like the fact that when I step on a train in Glasgow and I step off the train somewhere else, I hear a different language, a different sound system, and I find that interesting.'

Task A

1 Make rough notes on how much you agree with Tom Leonard and why you think that way. Then make a list of all of the regional accents you can name.

2 Copy and complete the grid below to collect some evidence for your assessment task. Ask up to four friends what they think of people who speak with different accents and why. Be sure to include a reason for each opinion.

Accent	Friend 1	Friend 2	Friend 3	Friend 4
Cockney (London)				
Geordie (Northeast England)				
Merseyside				
Glaswegian				
West Yorkshire				
Standard English/Received Pronunciation BBC newsreader				

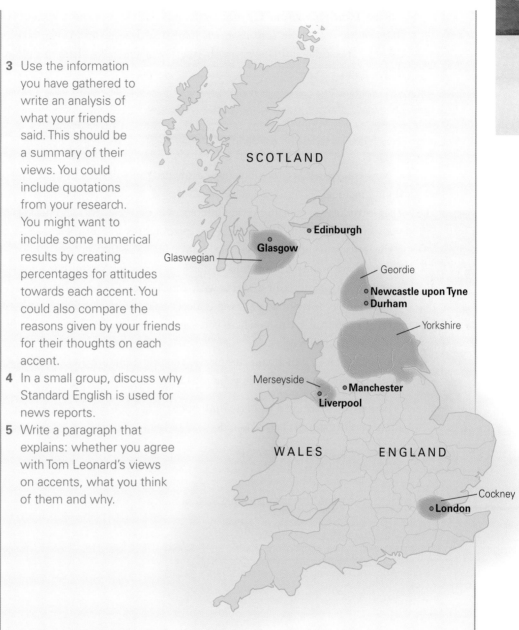

3 Use the information you have gathered to write an analysis of what your friends said. This should be a summary of their views. You could include quotations from your research. You might want to include some numerical results by creating percentages for attitudes towards each accent. You could also compare the reasons given by your friends for their thoughts on each accent.

4 In a small group, discuss why Standard English is used for news reports.

5 Write a paragraph that explains: whether you agree with Tom Leonard's views on accents, what you think of them and why.

SCOTLAND

Edinburgh

Glasgow

Glaswegian

Geordie

Newcastle upon Tyne
Durham

Yorkshire

Merseyside

Manchester
Liverpool

WALES

ENGLAND

Cockney

London

When you are discussing the task in your small groups, make sure you get your friends to explain their thoughts. This will give you detailed evidence to include in your response and will make it sound more authoritative.

Read 'Checking out me History' by John Agard. It is in the new *AQA Anthology: Moon on the Tides*. Like Tom Leonard, John Agard writes in his natural accent and dialect. This time it is Guyanan. In the poem, he talks about his West Indian background.

Task B

In groups, discuss what John Agard is saying about himself and his heritage in 'Checking out me History'. Make notes on the words he uses and how he makes his points.

Now you are ready to begin your assessment. You will need to write a piece which should include:

- an introduction explaining the differences between accents and dialects
- a section explaining how people are regarded because of their accents and why this is so; you should use evidence from your research data here
- your views on how accents affect your view of people; you might want to include how much you agree or disagree with Tom Leonard's thoughts here
- a section on how our accents and dialects establish our identities and sometimes resist conformity; this is where you can use your evidence from your discussion of John Agard's work
- a conclusion in which you summarise your thoughts, including what you think other people might think of your accent

Remember: this task is about analysing and explaining. Keep your focus on how to make your readers understand what you want them to know.

Before you start, you should think about what you want your reader to know about accents and dialects. Then decide how you will get that into your answer.

Task C

Copy and complete the grid below to help you plan your assessment. The first one is done for you but you can choose your own way of doing it. You will need to add more sections of your own.

What you want the reader to know	Where it comes in the assessment
The difference between accents and dialects	In the introduction
Some examples of accents and dialect words	
What people think about accents and dialects	
How accents and dialects can affect our lives	

Grade descriptors for this assessment task are outlined in the table below.

Grade A	A perceptive analysis of how you and other people use and regard accents using sophisticated interpretation, analysis and evaluations of your key data.
Grade C	A confident explanation of how you and others use and regard accents including analysis of your data and of public attitudes to spoken language variations.
Grade F	A response which shows some awareness of how you and others use and regard accents including some understanding of your data and some awareness of public attitudes to spoken language variations.

Student response to assessment task

A report out this week says that accents and dialects could be affecting some people's job prospects. It suggests that accents, which are the way words sound, and dialect words, which are used in some areas of the country but not others, affect our views about the people who use them. The report suggests that everyone should use Standard English when they speak or Received Pronunciation, as it is also known. Is this true? Should everyone speak as if they are reading the news? What if you don't? In response to the report, I have made a series of investigations and discovered a number of startling revelations…

Examiner's comment

The candidate has linked the task to a real world activity, thus looking at spoken language outside the classroom setting. The main findings of the report are given in a brief summary which leads into a series of rhetorical questions. This draws the readers into the assignment and makes them consider their own reactions to the subject. By using the phrase 'startling revelations' the candidate is deliberately choosing language that will create interest in the readers and make them want to know what the revelations are. This maintains the readers' attention and paves the way for a logical sequence of explanations. This candidate has achieved all the necessary requirements for a Grade C opening.

How to improve

The answer would benefit from a more interesting opening. Using a rhetorical question to draw the reader into it would help as it would increase the reader's interest.

How can you improve your grade?

This task has two distinct sections which require different skills. You should ask yourself the following questions while doing the research part:

- Am I finding out enough about accents and dialects to enable me to explain clearly what people think about them?
- Have I found information from anywhere outside the classroom? Have I done research at home, for instance by asking my parents or grandparents what they think, to get views across different age ranges?
- Have I decided on what I think about accents and dialects?

Remember: make sure you have enough information to enable you to write 800–1,000 words.

In the written response, you should ask yourself the following questions:

- Have I explained clearly what the differences are between accents and dialects?
- Have I included evidence from my friends and from other people?
- Have I included quotations from people?
- Have I referred to the poems of John Agard and Tom Leonard?
- Have I given my personal views?

> **Remember:** you need to make your response individual, even though you may have shared some aspects of your research with your friends. This means that you must tell your audience what *you* think.

As part of your research, you might want to try to find information on the internet. An interesting website to start with is **www.soundcomparisons.com** which features audio clips of people from different regions saying the same words in their own accents. It also has examples of English being spoken by Americans, Australians, Canadians and South Africans.

Another website that you might find useful is **www.bbc.co.uk/voices/recordings/index.shtml** which contains voices from throughout the country in real conversations. They play in BBC Media Player. You might need to open the audio clips in another window to hear them.

Spoken genres

Assessment task

Discuss the use of language in advertising and write an explanation of your findings.

What does the task expect you to do? At first sight, it seems simple. You only have to do two things:

- discuss
- write

> **Remember:** advertisers are trying to persuade you to do something. The work you do on writing to persuade will help you here.

However, there are many hidden sections to this task. You cannot discuss without doing some research and you need to have evidence of your research. This will form the data for your assessment.

You also need to be clear about what your data are for. They should not just be a list of what is said in advertisements. Your data should help you to explain why it is being said, who the advertisements are aimed at and the effect the advertisements will have.

This assessment is about spoken language, so you will only really need to examine advertising on television or radio, although you could comment on cinema or internet advertising too.

Task A

At home, watch television or listen to the radio. Choose three advertisements from each and write down what they say about the product they are advertising. Copy and complete the grids below to help you structure your notes.

Television

Product	What advert says
1	
2	
3	

Radio

Product	What advert says
1	
2	
3	

Are there any similarities between the language that is used in advertisements on television and radio? What are the differences? What words did the advertisers use to encourage you to buy their products? Did you hear any of the words below?

Value for money

DOUBLE DISCOUNT

BARGAIN

CRAZY PRICES

BEST EVER

EVERYTHING MUST GO

These prices can't last

SALE ENDS MONDAY

BOGOF BUY 1, GET 1 FREE

HURRY WHILE STOCKS LAST

FOR **1** DAY ONLY

BUY NOW PAY NOTHING 'TIL NEXT YEAR

Task B

Work with a partner.

1 Discuss how the words above might influence people to buy a product. Focus on the words and on their effect on the audience.

2 Share your information about the advertisements you researched for Task A with your partner. Concentrate on what is being said in the advertisements. Discuss how the language affects the audience and if you can tell who the target audience is by the language that is being used or the way the words are being said.

3 Discuss which advertisements are most likely to influence you to buy a product.

You will need to record your thoughts/discussions as they will provide extra data for your assessment.

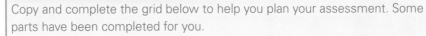

7

Assessment for Learning

When you are discussing, make sure you get your friends to explain their thoughts. This will give you detailed evidence to include in your response and will make it sound more authoritative. Ask your friends how clearly you have explained your thoughts and what parts are not clear.

Task C

Copy and complete the grid below to help you plan your assessment. Some parts have been completed for you.

Note: You do not have to follow this grid. You can make your own instead — the most successful assessments are often the most original.

Section	Content
Opening	Where do we find advertising and what is it trying to do?
Radio and television	Why are these media used for advertising?
Examples of advertisements: how do they try to persuade the audience to buy?	
Target audiences: how can we tell from the language that is being used?	
Personal views on which language would influence you to buy a product	
Conclusion: how effective is language use in advertisements?	

Remember: focus on the language of the advertisements. How are the advertisers using language to achieve their aims?

Remember: 1,000 words telling your reader what happens in a series of advertisements will not gain you many marks. This assessment is about explaining. The work you have done on writing to explain will help you here.

Grade descriptors for this assessment task are outlined in the table below.

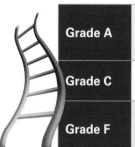

Grade A	A perceptive analysis of how you and other people respond to the language used in advertisements using sophisticated interpretation, analysis and evaluations of your key data.
Grade C	A confident explanation of how you and others respond to the language used in advertisements including analysis of your data.
Grade F	A response which shows some awareness of how you and others respond to the language used in advertisements including some understanding of your data.

Student response to assessment task

Opening

Do you want to buy a three piece suite? No, I don't either but I do know where I can get one and how much it will cost me. I don't want to buy double glazing either but I can tell you where you'll get the best offer in town, with free fitting and a ten year guarantee thrown in at no extra cost! How can I do this? Am I a mystic clairvoyant with magical powers who can predict market trends with ease? Perhaps I have a part-time job on yell.com. Have I gone the whole hog and swallowed and inwardly digested the entire contents of Yellow Pages? No, it's none of these. It's quite simple really. I'm a teenager and I watch television.

That's it. There's no great secret. I watch television and that makes me an expert on everything from frozen food to Ford Fiestas. Like all of us, I am assaulted in my own home by advertisers who try to persuade me to buy their goods in preference to someone else's identical product. Partly to escape the adverts and partly to escape Coronation Street, I often go to my room and go on the internet. They're there again! Silently sneaking through my system, infiltrating my broadband defences, the little rascals appear on my screen. They slide up the side, telling me to get fit or get fat, to buy this or buy that. Is there no escape? Where are my headphones? I'll listen to the radio instead. Oh no, they're here again! Jolly jingles that bruise my brain. I haven't the slightest interest in who is the best builder's merchant in the country and I'll probably never need to know but whoever it is, I'm singing their song!

Examiner's comment

The candidate has approached the task in a very individual way. You are in no doubt that the views expressed are the candidate's own. However, they are delivered in such a way that the reader can relate to them. The use of rhetorical questions pushes the reader into agreeing with the candidate's feelings. The style of the response is witty and satirical, using alliteration and rhyme to deliberately create an effect. This candidate has achieved all the necessary requirements for a Grade A opening.

However, the assignment is about explaining the effect of the language being used in advertising. Although this opening has done that it has concentrated on the candidate's response. It has not given any specific examples or analysis.

How to improve

In order to maintain the high grade, the candidate would need to focus for the rest of the assessment on the words used by advertisers and how they achieve their effects.

Assessment for Learning

Deliver your assessment to some friends in draft form. Ask them whether you have got the balance right between opinions, evidence and analysis and where you need to make changes.

Student response to assessment task

Explanation

I don't think advertising has much effect on me, yet it must have. If not, how would I know that 'Beanz means Heinz', 'the ultimate driving experience' is a BMW or that 'Mums go to Iceland'? I'm as much a victim of the language of advertising as everybody else. Sometimes, it's not what is said, it's what is implied that gets the message across. When the producers talk about the 'Lynx effect', I know exactly what they mean and start heading for the bathroom cupboard. Somebody is going to be lucky tonight! You see, advertisers prey upon our weaknesses. They understand our insecurities and desires and they feed off them. They know we don't necessarily *want* their products but the words they use make us *need* them. We can't help it. Who can resist BOGOF (buy one, get one free); or 20% less fat; or a double discount? When I hear the words, 'Hurry, this is a limited offer while stocks last. When they're gone, they're gone', I'm almost rushing to the shops without listening to what it is I'm supposed to be buying.

I guess I'm an advert junkie. I know what they're trying to do but I still fall for it. I'm back every 30 minutes for my fix of bargains and special offers. 'Our best ever' makes my pulse quicken and sweat break out on my brow. 'All this for less than a tenner!' Yes, I know it's £9.99 but I can't resist. My brain tells me it's stupid, that it's just advertising talk but…I want it. I need it. I have to have it!

Examiner's comment

The candidate has begun to analyse the effects of the language used in advertising by portraying the audience as innocent victims and showing the impact the words have on them by implying that everyone would have the same reaction. There are many personal responses in this which show that the candidate clearly understands the effect of the language used. The style is personal and engaging. The use of the pronoun 'you' draws the reader into the text and maintains the interest because the reader starts to associate with the candidate's thoughts. The candidate adopts a persona and maintains it throughout this piece, managing to include both humour and a feeling of desperation. Grade C candidates would just use quotations and say what effect they have on the audience. This candidate takes a more sophisticated approach, indicating clearly how the advertisements work through interpretation, analysis and evaluation of the key data which is shown through the reactions created. If the response continued in this manner it would be awarded a Grade A.

> **How to improve**
> The candidate needs to expand on the opinions being given here to take account of the views of other people.

How can you improve your grade?

This task has two distinct sections which require different skills. You should ask yourself the following questions while doing your research:

- Am I finding enough evidence about the language of advertisements or am I just describing what happens in them?
- Have I found any information about how advertisements influence people from anywhere outside the classroom, for instance by asking my friends, parents or grandparents what they think?
- Have I expressed the effect language in advertising has on me?

> **Remember:** make sure you have enough information to write 800–1,000 words.

When completing the written response section, you should ask yourself the following questions:

- Have I explained clearly what advertisers are trying to do?
- Have I included evidence from advertisements and explained what the advertisers are trying to do and how they do it?
- Have I included responses from other people?
- Have I given my personal views?

> **Remember:** you need to make your response individual, even though you may have shared some aspects of your research with your friends. This means that you must tell your audience what *you* think.

Multi-modal task

This final task is perhaps the most difficult because it is the most different from any assessments that have been set before. It requires you to study ways in which new technologies blur traditional distinctions between speaking and writing, and to show how online identities are created and how online talk is potentially ambiguous.

This means that the assessment must be based around electronic communications which will include video-phoning, texting, e-mail, MSN and social networking sites like Facebook and Twitter. Your data for this assessment could include printouts of electronic messages or transcripts of video-phone conversations. The aim is to show how these forms of communication are changing the way we use language.

> **Assessment task**
>
> Research and explain how new technologies link both text and speech and how they can be used.

What does the task expect you to do? At first sight, it seems really difficult. You have to:

- research new technologies
- analyse how they work and their effects
- present your findings to an audience

> **Remember:** this is a new task. You may well know more about it than your teachers. Most of it will need your opinions rather than facts and a lot of your evidence could be anecdotal.

Task A

My Space, Facebook and Twitter are three online social networking sites. List any others you can think of. You may never have used any of them. In groups, discuss how many of you use them, and what for. Discuss how MSN Messenger is used. It's almost like talking but it is not. Discuss how it is different. You might want to do this online and print it out as part of your data.

Assessment for Learning

When you are discussing, make sure you get your friends to explain their thoughts. This will give you detailed evidence to include in your response. Make sure you discuss the language that is used in electronic communication. Talk about how it is different from speech and why. If you have never used a social networking site, get someone who has to explain to you how they work.

In August 2009 the Roman Catholic Archbishop of Westminster, Vincent Nichols, made the following comments.

> Archbishop Nichols said that communicating via social networking sites and mobile phones rather than meeting face to face was 'dehumanising' community life. He believed it was weakening relationships.
>
> 'There's a worry that an excessive use or an almost exclusive use of text and e-mails means that as a society we're losing some of the ability to build interpersonal communication that's necessary for living together and building a community.
>
> 'We are losing social skills, the human interaction skills, how to read a person's mood, to read their body language and how to be patient until the moment is right to make or press a point.
>
> 'Too much exclusive use of electronic information dehumanises what is a very, very important part of community life and living together.'

Task B

Read the archbishop's comments and discuss with a partner how realistic you think his views are. Why are you more likely to misinterpret or misunderstand what someone has written than what someone says directly to you? Make notes on this and include them as part of your evidence.

Task C

Copy and complete the grid below to help you plan your assessment.
Some parts have been completed for you.

Note: You do not have to follow this
grid. You can make your own instead —
the most successful assessments
are often the most original.

Remember: focus on how
the language is being used.

Remember: this
assessment is
about explaining
and exploring your
ideas. The work you
do on writing to
explain and inform
will help you here.

Section	Content
Opening	What are the new technologies and who might use them?
Texting	How is the language of texting different from normal speech and why?
MSN	How has texting led to other forms of electronic communication and what are their uses?
How to set up an account and establish identities with other users	
Possible problems	
Conclusion: how technology has changed language and what further changes you think might take place as a result of it	

Grade descriptors for this assessment task are outlined in the table below.

Grade A	A perceptive analysis of how language is used in different situations using sophisticated interpretation, analysis and evaluations of your key data.
Grade C	A confident explanation of how language is used in different situations including analysis of your data.
Grade F	A response which shows some awareness of how language is used in different situations including some understanding of your data.

Student response to assessment task

Opening

New technology. The words make my grandma shiver. She hates mobile phones and thinks texting should be banned because it encourages us, as she says, to 'talk wrong'. She thinks Twitter is what birds do, Facebook is a pictorial phone book, and My Space is next to Outer Space. To be honest, until I started doing this project, I agreed with her on most of that. What's wrong with just using the phone and talking? Well, there's the cost. If you've got broadband all the internet is virtually free. Also, you can break off in the middle of a conversation, go to the toilet and just pick up the thread when you come back. That's slightly more difficult on the phone.

Until I did this, I'd never used a social networking site so thanks go to Rachel for showing me how. Now my social life has improved no end. I've got lots of new friends I've never met and I've learned a whole new language. I've also found a new way of putting off doing homework while I'm pretending to be doing it! Why *read* poems from different cultures when I can *talk* directly to someone from one? Once you get into this style of communication, the world is your oyster. There are no barriers. Without it, the world is your lobster.

Examiner's comment

This is a confident introduction. It is a personal response which expresses the candidate's thoughts clearly and explains them well. There are clear 'before' and 'after' sessions which show the effect on the candidate. The introduction concentrates on scene setting. It does not include any details of the uses of the new technologies although it hints at this in the reference to 'different cultures'. The ending of this section uses a cliché but is still effective. This opening would achieve a high Grade C.

How to improve

The candidate needs to show more analysis of how language has changed over time.

Texting

I suppose the beginning of this communication revolution was with the introduction of the mobile phone and the consequent ability of everyone in the nation to be able to send text messages to each other. Texting was quicker than calling. You didn't have to make a connection and wait for someone to answer after rummaging through their pockets or bags for the phone. Frequently this sent you to their answer phones and you left a message. The commonsense thing to do was to cut out the middle man and just send them the message, particularly if you were in a place where it was difficult to phone. Often these texts would be short and sometimes sent over a short distance, for instance from underneath one desk to another in lessons!

The attraction was probably the speed and convenience but writing out everything in Standard English defeats all of that so text language evolved. Typing on a phone is laborious and time consuming so people made up short cuts. We all know what they mean but they are just quicker. Here are some examples:

m8 = mate

imo = in my opinion

2day = today

Often the vowels are missed out. Try working out what this means:

wre ws u lst nte

You can all read and understand it. So is it any worse than Standard English? I don't think so. It's just different and frightening to some people because they aren't used to it.

Did you notice any problems in my example? Well, for a start there's no punctuation so it can be difficult to work out where sentences end. Also, the 'l' in 'lst' looks very like the number 1 so you might have struggled to work out it said last not first — that would create a whole different meaning to the text.

Examiner's comment

The candidate has shown some examples of how language is being used and changed. In addition the candidate is beginning to look at some of the possible ambiguities and problems of texting. This response has a personal style but the content is not very original. Many students will provide similar details and opinions. As a result of the confidence of the writing, the use of examples and the explanation, this section would achieve a high Grade C.

How to improve

The candidate needs to demonstrate more analysis of data and to explain his or her thoughts clearly.

Problems

So, is it all plain sailing into the glorious horizon of a bright orange technological future? Unfortunately, no. Not everyone is in favour of social networking. Teachers and parents may well regard it as a waste of time that drags their children away from their studies. They should be grateful. Sometimes the only way my parents talk to me is through MSN. I get messages sent up to my bedroom: 'Your tea is ready.' It's really handy.

Some people think there is a darker, more dangerous, perhaps even sinister side to social networking. We can't see or hear the people we are 'talking' with. How do we know that they are genuine? How do we know our new 'friends' really are just that, friends? The Roman Catholic Archbishop of Westminster, Vincent Nichols, said, 'We are losing social skills, the human interaction skills, how to read a person's mood, to read their body language and how to be patient until the moment is right to make or press a point.' I looked up the whole of the article on the web. It suggests that electronic relationships can leave young people in a mess when they end and could even lead to suicide. The archbishop isn't the only one with reservations. Just type social networking sites into Google and see what you get. It's not all bad news though. Computerweekly.com said, 'Online social networking is now more important than print advertising for finding IT staff.' So, if you want a job, get an account.

Examiner's comment

The candidate makes clear references to his or her own research and data. The data are not particularly analysed. Instead they are stated with open-ended comments afterwards, leaving the listeners make up their own minds. It is not always clear what the candidate's views are but they are clearly personal ones. The style is engaging, but the lack of analysis restricts this response to a high Grade C.

How can you improve your grade?

This task has two distinct sections which require different skills. You should ask yourself the following questions while doing your research:

- Am I finding enough evidence about the new technologies and how they are being used or am I just naming them?
- Have I found any information about how much the new technologies are being used, for instance by asking my friends, parents or grandparents what they think?
- Have I found out anything about the way the new technologies are changing language use?
- Have I found out anything about the dangers of such sites?

Remember: make sure you have enough information to enable you to write 800–1,000 words.

Speaking and listening

In the written response, you should ask yourself the following questions:

- Have I explained clearly what the new technologies are and how they work?
- Have I included evidence in the form of transcripts of conversations?
- Have I included responses from other people?
- Have I examined the problems of using new technology?
- Have I given my personal views?

Remember: you need to give your thoughts and opinions. This means that you must tell your audience what *you* think.

Remember: the key with all the assignments relating to AO2 is to make sure that you do some research. Without this you will not be able to explain. This will require you to call on your reading and writing skills, as well as your speaking and listening ones.

Chapter 8

Responding to literature

Your reading in English Literature will be assessed against the following Assessment Objectives (AOs).

AO1	• Respond to texts **critically** and **imaginatively**; **select** and **evaluate** relevant textual detail to **illustrate** and **support** interpretations.
AO2	• Explain how **language**, **structure** and **form** contribute to writers' **presentation** of **ideas**, **themes** and **settings**.
AO3	• Make **comparisons** and explain **links** between texts, evaluating writers' different ways of **expressing meaning** and **achieving effects**.
AO4	• Relate texts to their **social**, **cultural** and **historical contexts**; explain how texts have been **influential** and **significant** to self and other readers in different contexts and at different times.

The specification

There are two different routes through the English Literature specification: Route A and Route B. Ask your teacher which route you are taking. Note that Unit 1 is compulsory for both routes.

Route A		Route B
Unit 1: exploring modern texts *External examination: 1 hour 30 minutes (40%)* Section A: modern prose or drama Section B: exploring cultures		Unit 1: exploring modern texts *External examination: 1 hour 30 minutes (40%)* Section A: modern prose or drama Section B: exploring cultures
Unit 2: poetry across time *External examination: 1 hour 15 minutes (35%)* Section A: poetry cluster from the anthology Section B: responding to an unseen poem	**OR**	Unit 4: approaching Shakespeare and the English Literary Heritage *External examination: 1 hour 15 minutes (35%)* Section A: Shakespeare Section B: prose from the English Literary Heritage
Unit 3: the significance of Shakespeare and the English Literary Heritage *Controlled assessment: 3–4 hours (25%)*		Unit 5: exploring poetry *Controlled assessment: 3–4 hours (25%)*

No matter which piece of literature you are writing about, you need broadly the same set of skills. The reading skills required are, as we noted in Chapter 1, very similar to those assessed in the English and English Language courses. In addition, if you are going to write about 'language, structure and form' you need to be able to use the appropriate technical terms which apply to poetry, prose and drama.

Key grade criteria for each AO

Grade A	AO1	An enthusiastic and critical response to texts, showing alternative approaches and interpretations, integrating references to support their views.
	AO2	A confident exploration and evaluation of how language, structure and form contribute to achieve different effects on readers.
	AO3	Illuminating comparisons and connections made between texts.
	AO4	Identification and comment on the impact of the social, cultural and historical contexts on different readers at different times.

Grade C	AO1	A clear understanding of how writers use ideas, themes and settings in texts to affect the reader, referring to textual detail to support views.
	AO2	A personal response to the effects of language, structure and form, referring to textual detail to support views.
	AO3	An explanation of the relevance and impact of connections and comparisons.
	AO4	Show awareness of some of the social, cultural and historical contexts and how this influences meanings for today's readers.
Grade F	AO1	Can show some awareness of key ideas, themes and form in texts with reference to significant features or details.
	AO2	A personal response to the effects of language, structure and form in texts.
	AO3	Straightforward connections and comparisons between texts.
	AO4	Awareness of some aspects of how texts relate to their specific social, cultural and historical contexts.

How can you improve your grade?

You can improve your grade by addressing the four Assessment Objectives.

AO	Key words	What the key words mean
AO1	**respond to texts critically and imaginatively**	You work out what the text means for you: you do not just write down what you have been taught. You think for yourself.
	select and evaluate relevant textual detail to illustrate and support interpretations	You use textual evidence to back up what you have to say.
AO2	**explain how language, structure and form contribute to writers' presentation of ideas, themes and settings**	You explain how the choices that a writer makes about words, shape and how a text looks influence the reader.
AO3	**make comparisons and explain links between texts**	You can see similarities and differences between texts.
	evaluating writers' different ways of expressing meaning and achieving effects	You show how writers do things similarly and differently.
AO4	**relate texts to their social, cultural and historical contexts; explain how texts have been influential and significant to self and other readers in different contexts and at different times**	You show how texts fit into a particular place, time and culture and how they may reflect or influence that contextual background.

AO1 and AO2

AO1: respond to texts critically and imaginatively; select and evaluate relevant textual detail to illustrate and support interpretations

AO2: explain how language, structure and form contribute to writers' presentation of ideas, themes and settings

Task A

Read the poem entitled 'The Tyger'.

The Tyger

Tyger! Tyger! burning bright
In the forests of the night,
What immortal hand or eye
Could frame thy fearful symmetry?

In what distant deeps or skies
Burnt the fire of thine eyes?
On what wings dare he aspire?
What the hand, dare seize the fire?

And what shoulder, and what art,
Could twist the sinews of thy heart?
And when thy heart began to beat,
What dread hand? And what dread feet?

What the hammer? What the chain?
In what furnace was thy brain?
What the anvil? What dread grasp
Dare its deadly terrors clasp?

When the stars threw down their spears,
And water'd heaven with their tears,
Did he smile his work to see?
Did he who made the Lamb make thee?

Tyger! Tyger! burning bright
In the forests of the night,
What immortal hand or eye
Dare frame thy fearful symmetry?

William Blake (1794)

Task B

1 Try to respond imaginatively by writing down what you understand by the following words in 'The Tyger':
   - Tyger
   - bright
   - night
   - dread
   - fearful
   - burning
   - forests
   - water'd
   - Lamb
   - symmetry

2 Many of these words can have positive or negative connotations. Copy and complete the following table to sort the words into three columns: positive; negative; neutral. The table has been started for you, but you might disagree with these choices.

Positive	Negative	Neutral
bright	fearful	symmetry

Remember: the ability to 'show alternative approaches and interpretations' is an A-grade skill.

Task C

What are the connotations of the first two lines of 'The Tyger'?

Student response to Task C

The writer is almost shouting to the tiger in the first two words 'Tyger! Tyger!' as if he is wanting to attract the tiger's attention. I think that the tiger is very colourful and bright with the poet drawing attention to these words by starting them with the same letter and he also rhymes 'bright' with the word 'night' which has another, very different connotation. Maybe the poet is saying that the tiger has two sides to it.

Examiner's comment

The student is beginning to say something interesting about the connotations of words and ideas in these opening lines. Had these ideas been developed, then there would have been a clear understanding. At the moment, there is only 'some awareness of key ideas': an F-grade skill.

How to improve

Develop every idea, rather than simply identifying features.

Assessment for Learning

Write a C-grade response or above, in which you develop each of the following points:

- The way the poet addresses the tiger directly.
- Explore in more detail the connotations of the alliterative phrase 'burning bright'.
- How does this link with 'night'?
- What are the connotations of the word 'forest'?
- 'Symmetry' is obviously a key word for this stanza: what are its connotations in the light of what you have written?

AO3

Make comparisons and explain links between texts, evaluating writers' different ways of expressing meaning and achieving effects

Task A

Look at Blake's original illustrated version of 'The Tyger'.

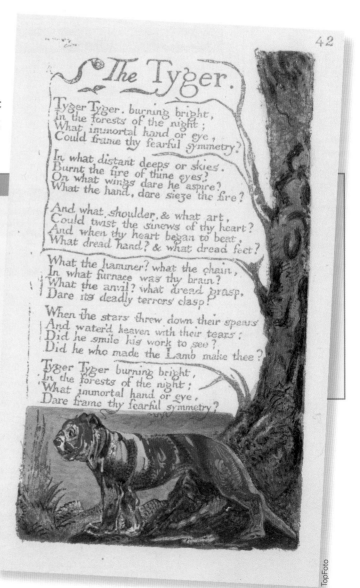

Task B

Compare (AO3) 'how structure and form contribute to writers' presentation of ideas and themes' (AO2) in 'The Tyger'. Copy and complete the following table to help you structure your response.

	Tyger (version 1)	Tyger (version 2)
Structure (the way the different parts relate to each other)	The tiger looks more threatening at the side	It looks less important at the bottom of the page
Form (the shape or the way it is presented on the page)	The tiger is ready to pounce, so it complements the shape of the poem	The handwriting (calligraphy) makes the poem less harsh

Task C

1 What do you think the poet is saying about God and religion in 'The Tyger'?
2 How would that fit in with the 'social, cultural and historical contexts' (AO4) of this poem?
3 How does this view fit in with what we think about God and tigers in today's Britain? (AO4)

Remember: you do not earn many marks for simply telling the story of a text: most marks are awarded for answering the question and addressing the Assessment Objectives.

Student response to Task C

I think the writer is asking questions about God and the nature of creation. I believe that he is asking fundamental questions about the sort of being that could create and 'twist the sinews of thy heart'.

Blake was writing during a period of great change in Britain and Europe as a whole. Within Britain, the Industrial Revolution was making a lot of people question their beliefs as they lived in environments where the 'hammer', 'chain' and 'anvil' were more commonplace. Blake, I think, was saying that some greater being, or God, created such marvellous and 'fearful' creatures.

However, Blake is hardly sure of his ground. There are many questions in this poem, and I do not think that they are rhetorical. I believe that Blake is asking fundamental questions about which he is not himself certain. He had some strange, non-conformist views about religion and this poem hints at a different view of creation, heaven and earth, when he states:

> 'When the stars threw down their spears,
> And water'd heaven with their tears'

This hints at a very visual perception of heaven and earth, hence the visual images to accompany his poem...

Examiner's comment

This is an enthusiastic, committed, exploratory and illuminating response by a student who is showing evidence of what she is learning: not what she has been taught. It is clearly of A-grade standard and is as illuminating for the examiner as it is for the student.

How to improve

Use even more words like: 'I think' and 'hints', which alert the examiner to an exploratory line of thought.

Task D

Explain how the language used by the poet in 'The Tyger' relates this text to its historical context.

Note: Use the table that you completed for Task B to help you answer this question.

Student response to Task D

There are many aspects of this poem which place it firmly within its historical context. Blake published this poem in 1794 and there are several clues that help the reader to place the poem both historically and culturally. I am going to focus on two aspects: the lexis and the rhyme scheme.

Many of the words in this poem date the poem both by meaning and the way they are spelt. The most obvious example is the title. Most modern anthologies maintain Blake's choice of the spelling 'tyger' which was already a little old-fashioned, or archaic, when he wrote the poem. He must therefore have spelt the word in this way on purpose for effect.

The effect is immediate as the poet repeats the words almost like a song. This poem is taken from Blake's *Songs of Experience* and there are many songlike aspects to the poem which I will refer to later. However, this pointedly archaic spelling of a word makes the reader think about its overall meaning within the poem. The spelling would suggest that the concept of 'The Tyger' is metaphorical. We are not meant to think of some god creating a tyger in his 'dread grasp', but we are meant to think of what the tyger actually stands for within Blake's overall thought processes.

I think that it is a metaphor for industrialisation which could certainly be supported by the number of words to do with this process. Another way of putting this is a restricted semantic code. For example, here is a cursory list of all the words within the semantic field of industrialisation: 'fire', 'hammer', 'chain', 'furnace' and 'anvil'. There is an almost Promethean aspect to the way fire was seized, in the same way that Prometheus first seized fire from the gods. So it may not be wholly Christian in culture. Interesting!

The second aspect I would like to explore is the poem's rhyme scheme which clearly points to this poem being part of a series of songs...

Examiner's comment

This response shows clear evidence of 'a confident exploration and evaluation of how language contributes to achieve different effects on readers' within a historical and cultural background. The nearer that a candidate actually gets to satisfying an Assessment Objective then the higher the grade achieved. This is another example of an A/B-grade response with the sort of conceptualisation required to earn such a grade.

Assessment for Learning

Reread this student's answer and identify the words that show that this student is working at a 'conceptualised level'. Copy and complete the following table to structure your answer.

Sophisticated vocabulary	Evidence of conceptualisation

Exchange your table with a partner and discuss your findings.

AO4

Relate texts to their social, cultural and historical contexts; explain how texts have been influential and significant to self and other readers in different contexts and at different times

Key words	What the key words mean
relate	This means to make a link, or association, with something else.
social	This relates to the ways that people form groups or live together.
cultural	This means those things which are considered to be important artistically or socially.
historical	This is concerned with a study of the past.
influential	This means having an effect on another person.

Where is AO4 assessed?

This AO is assessed in Unit 1 (exploring modern texts) under examination conditions.

Note: If you are only taking GCSE English, then you can use this section to prepare for the exploring cultures aspect of Unit 3 (understanding and producing creative texts), where Steinbeck is one of the named authors in the suggested list.

How is AO4 assessed?

This will be assessed via one question on the set text that you have studied. The question will be in two parts. The first part (a) will ask you to respond to a passage from the text. The second part (b) will ask you to link the passage to the whole text.

There will be 30 marks for this question, which translates to 20% of your overall English Literature mark

Note that all the Assessment Objectives are examined in this question. AO4 is not assessed in isolation. Nor is it assessed by asking you to tell the story.

Sample exam question

John Steinbeck: *Of Mice and Men*

Read the passage and then answer the questions which follow:

Extract: description of Crooks' room on the first 2 pages of Part Four, up to: 'Noiselessly, Lennie appeared in the open doorway…'

(a) How do the details in this passage add to your understanding of Crooks?

(b) How does Steinbeck use the character of Crooks in the novel as a whole to convey ideas about America in the 1930s?

Task A

Read the sample exam question above. Copy it down and highlight what it is actually asking you to do.

Task B

Copy and complete the following table to help you answer part (a) of the exam question.

Detail	How it adds to your understanding of Crooks
'And he had books, too…'	
'for, being alone,'	

Student response to Task B

Detail	How it adds to your understanding of Crooks
'And he had books, too....'	This shows us that Crooks was more permanent, so he had more possessions than the white men on the farm. Also, he can read which might contradict some cultural prejudices that some may have. Finally, there is a variety of books which shows that he has many interests and needs.

Examiner's comment

This response, in note form, is already addressing two of the four Assessment Objectives (AO1 and AO4) and would just need development and further exemplification to gain a C grade.

How to improve

Write this answer out and add more detail. For example:

• What other possessions did Crooks own?

• What importance did reading books, or magazines, have in the rest of the book?

• What do the types of books suggest about Crooks and his style of life?

Task C

Answer part (b) of the exam question, making sure that you address the other two Assessment Objectives (AO2 and AO3) which require you to make comparisons and 'explain how language, structure and form contribute to writers' presentation of ideas, themes and settings'. This is always the hardest AO to address.

Student response to Task C

Just about all the characters in this novel are portrayed as 'types' in order to allow the writer to comment on his views about the social and historical background against which this novel is set. Crooks is included to give a view about the way that black Americans were treated at the time. This is obvious later in this particular passage of the book and elsewhere when Crooks interacts with the other characters.

For example, Steinbeck shows how Crooks' position within the farm hierarchy is extremely precarious. First, he realises that he has gone too far with his goading of Lennie when he 'walked dangerously towards Crooks'. It almost seems that anyone and everyone can 'take after the nigger'. Candy related how one of the men, named Smitty, had beaten Crooks up the previous Christmas when they were all drunk and that it was only the fact that Crooks had a crooked back that saved him from further punishment.

Language is used throughout the novel to draw attention to the characters' attitude towards others, especially Crooks. He is routinely referred to as the 'nigger', in the same way that Curley's wife is never referred to by her name. It is Curley's wife who shows the truly precarious nature of Crooks' position on the farm, when she states: 'Well, you keep your place then, Nigger. I could get you strung up on a tree so easy it ain't even funny.'

The final part of the previous quotation is truly chilling in its repercussions. Crooks has to sleep out in the barn with the animals and is not allowed to mix socially with the other men, especially on their trips into town on a Saturday night. Crooks has to rely on his collection of 'dirty books' instead. Things were very different when Crooks was younger and he was always close to his two brothers on his father's chicken ranch.

The inclusion of Crooks as a representative of black Americans of the period gives Steinbeck the opportunity to portray not only the way that Crooks lived, but it also shows the reader what others thought about negroes at the time. Crooks knows his place, metaphorically in the manure heap, and the writer shows us several examples of the truth of this metaphor. Crooks is ostracised because Crooks realises the irony of having a room to himself with 'a manure pile under the window' and only Slim as an occasional visitor.

The whole horror of his position is only fully appreciated when Crooks is visited by the other three 'types' and Curley's wife firmly puts him in his place as mentioned earlier in the answer. 1930s America was not an enlightened time for civil rights and equality according to Steinbeck and this novel certainly exemplifies the deep divides.

Lennie, George and Candy

MGM/The Kobal Collection

Examiner's comment

This answer clearly shows an 'enthusiastic and critical response' and 'integrates references'. There is the beginnings of an 'exploration and evaluation of how language contributes to achieve different effects on the reader' and some 'illuminating connections' are made. The strongest aspect is the ability to 'identify and comment on the impact of the social and cultural contexts on different readers at different times'. These are all A-grade descriptors.

How to improve

Include more about the writer's use of language to give even more enlightenment about characterisation and how the writer uses form and structure to help to achieve his effects. Note how it is suggested that quite a lot can be gathered from the relatively short quotation in the chart for Task B in response to part (a) 'for, being alone'. If this passage is looked upon as a reading passage in the same way as non-fiction, or poetry, then the writer has made informed choices in order to try to affect the reader's response. What can be gathered just by paying attention to the punctuation in this quotation?

Task B

Now answer part (b) with reference to any, or all, of the following characters instead of Crooks:

- Curley's wife
- Lennie
- Candy

Controlled assessment task

Unit 3: the significance of Shakespeare and the English Literary Heritage

When you have studied your texts for Unit 3, you will be expected to consider the following key aspects:

- ideas, themes and issues
- characterisation
- settings

This controlled assessment is worth 25% of your overall English Literature mark, so you will be spending 25% of your available time for this subject on the topic that your teacher has chosen. The following task is just one example of many that could be studied.

Ingram

Sample assessment task

Compare the notion of 'hero' when applied to Macbeth in Shakespeare's play of the same name and Pip in *Great Expectations*.

Pip with Miss Havisham in the David Lean film of *Great Expectations*

Remember: you have to make links between the texts and you have to address the social, cultural and historical context.

Macbeth and Banquo meet the witches

Task A

Copy and complete the following table which contains some ideas for this assessment task.

Some definitions of the notion of what makes a 'hero':
- someone who commits heroic acts
- the main character in a work of fiction
- someone with superhuman skills/gifts
- ...

Remember: you do not get many marks for simply telling the story.

Macbeth	Great Expectations
He begins the play as a hero…	Pip begins the novel as a sort of hero when he befriends the convict…
Undoubtedly the main character because…. Macbeth also speaks in soliloquies…. This…	Also the main character as he is the narrator and it is in the first person…. This device…
Although Macbeth believes he has superhuman skills…	There are never any suggestions that Pip is superhuman, however, he does have a high regard for himself, for example…and he does win the fight with…

Task B

Copy and complete the following table to make sure that you address the social, cultural and historical aspects of each text in your answer.

	Macbeth	*Great Expectations*
Social	The notion of a 'hero' was mainly down to physical prowess…	Apart from Pip's fight, he was no hero, except when…
Cultural	Shakespeare wrote a lot of plays about 'heroes' because the concept was interesting to his audience, because…	Victorians were interested in heroes, but Pip is mainly interesting because he is the main character, therefore…
Historical	Although the story of Macbeth was an old one, it had relevance for Shakespeare's audiences because…	Dickens' readers were interested in whether someone could become socially mobile and…

Externally assessed: English Literature Unit 2

Literary Heritage plus Contemporary poetry, including comparative study

Where is this assessed?

There will be a choice of questions in Unit 2 on each of the sections of this externally assessed (examined) question. The four sections of poetry in the anthology are:

Characters and Voices

Conflict

Place

Relationships

They are in Section 1 of the anthology. You have to answer one question and you are advised to spend 45 minutes on this question, which will always be in two parts.

You should read one section in detail, in preparation for the examination, and one section in less detail in order to develop the skills of reading poetry (you will need these for the 'Unseen Poetry' section) and to satisfy the National Curriculum requirements. The following exercises are an ideal preparation to develop the requisite skills for this examination.

How is this assessed?

When you have studied your texts for this unit, you will be expected to consider the following key aspects:

> **how the poets use devices in order to enhance the meaning of their poems**

> **comparison of a named poem with another of your choice from the section you are answering**

> **what the poems are about, in your opinion**

This externally assessed unit is worth 35% of your overall English Literature mark, so you will be spending 35% of your time for this subject on the skills required.

Remember: you do not have to use a Literary Tradition poem (one written before 1914) to compare with the named poem in any given question: any poem from the named section will suffice.

Luckily your teacher will be an expert at this because the comparison of poetry has been an integral part of both English and English Literature for the past ten years. Because this book focuses on skills, poems from the previous anthology rather than the current one will be used as they are widely available and there is a lot of support material and knowledge within schools. This is also excellent preparation for the unseen peotry question (see Chapter 9).

Task A

Read the following poem and copy out the table that follows. Complete the table, which has been started for you, by writing notes to answer the question: How does Nichols present the effects of the hurricane and its effects upon her?

Hurricane Hits England

It took a hurricane, to bring her closer
To the landscape.
Half the night she lay awake,
The howling ship of the wind,
Its gathering rage,
Like some dark ancestral spectre.

Fotolia

Talk to me Huracan
Talk to me Oya
Talk to me Shango
And Hattie,
My sweeping, back-home cousin.

Tell me why you visit
An English coast?
What is the meaning
Of old tongues
Reaping havoc
In new places?

The blinding illumination,
Even as you short-
Circuit us
Into further darkness?

What is the meaning of trees
Falling heavy as whales
Their crusted roots
Their cratered graves?

Remember: look at the shape of a poem before you even read it. Poems are not just assessed for what they 'mean'. Simply 'telling the story' is a low level skill: it is the ability to explain why a poet has chosen: language, structure and form that gets you the marks.

O why is my heart unchained?
Tropical Oya of the Weather,
I am aligning myself to you,
I am following the movement of your winds,
I am riding the mystery of the storm.

Ah, sweet mystery,
Come to break the frozen lake in me,
Shaking the foundations of the very trees within me,
Come to let me know
That the earth is the earth is the earth.

Grace Nichols

The effects of the hurricane	Its effects upon her	Type of language used
The wind howled all night	It made her both fearful and reassured	Onomatopoeia e.g…
She tries to communicate directly with the hurricane	It makes her remember her cultural homeland in the Caribbean and Africa	Oya, Huracan, Shango

Task B

Use the notes in your table to answer the question: How does Nichols present the effects of the hurricane and its effects upon her?

Student response to Task B

At the beginning of the poem, the poet refers to a third person, 'her', to give the poem a universal appeal, rather than a personal response to this catastrophic weather event. The effects of the poem are mainly physical in nature in that the wind howls all night 'like some dark ancestral spectre', which makes her think of her ancestral roots in both the Caribbean and in Africa. The almost incantatory nature of lines 8–11 show that this weather event has several names and descriptions which are almost family names. The word 'cousin' also shows how the storm reminds her so much of her roots.

The poet even reverts to West Indian dialect in line 13 with these 'old tongues' creating so much devastation in this new home. 'The blinding illumination' comes about even when the electricity is off and in the midst of both literal and metaphorical 'darkness': the poet suddenly realises what is going on.

She draws attention to the line 'O why is my heart unchained?' by having it on a line by itself and she realises that her cultural background is clearly with 'Tropical Oya' as she mentally retraces her steps back to the Caribbean islands where hurricanes and high winds are a part of seasonal life. This geographically mis-placed tropical storm breaks 'the frozen lake in me', which represents her repressed love for her homeland and her cultural longings.

However, her last line successfully conveys that we are from one planet and that all cultures are inextricably linked:

'the earth is the earth is the earth.'

Only when it is read by an African Caribbean do we get the full meaning of this line as the word is pronounced 'eart' and we realise that the poet has concluded that it does not matter where you are in the world. We are all one in the sight of such forces of nature and these forces are linked in the same ways that people are. The definite conclusive 't' sound in the poem puts the matter beyond any doubt, as does the tri-fold repetition.

Examiner's comment

This is a clear example of a student who is beginning to 'conceptualise' and work out what he or she thinks the poet's big idea is. There is a clear understanding of how the poet has written the poem in order to try to explain to herself what she thinks has happened during this hurricane that so reminds her of home.

Another higher-order skill is the ability to integrate references within an answer, without quoting too much. Can you identify where this student is beginning to show evidence of this skill?

How to improve

What the answer lacks is a developed link between devices and conceptualisation (what the poet is 'on about'), which would have placed this answer more firmly in the A* band of marks. This is A*, but only just. When you work out what you think the concept is in a poem, then you have to find evidence to back up your ideas. Linking the 'what' and the 'how' together is the skill that gains the highest grades.

Assessment for Learning

Look again at the student's response and:
- identify where he or she has made these conceptualised thoughts
- suggest how he or she might have integrated some more telling references to devices in order to move it up a grade
- develop some of these points so that they show evidence of 'developing and sustaining'

Task C

Read the following poem and fill in the table that follows:

Patrolling Barnegat

Wild, wild the storm, and the high sea running.
Steady the roar of the gale, with incessant undertone muttering,
Shouts of demoniac laughter fitfully piercing and pealing,
Waves, air, midnight, their savagest trinity lashing,
Out in the shadows there milk-white combs careering,
On beachy slush and sand spirts of snow fierce slanting,
Where through the murk the easterly death-wind breasting,
Through cutting swirl and spray watchful and firm advancing,
(That in the distance! Is it a wreck? Is the red signal flaring?)
Slush and sand of the beach tireless till daylight wending,
Steadily, slowly, through hoarse roar never remitting,
Along the midnight edge by those milk-white combs careering,
A group of dim, weird forms, struggling, the night confronting,
That savage trinity warily watching.

Walt Whitman (1856)

Poetic devices	The effects they have on the reader
Repetition of '-ing' words on the ends of lines	
Repetition of 'Wild, wild...' at the beginning	
The grammatical strangeness of many of the lines, like: 'Waves, air, midnight, their savagest trinity lashing'	
The rule of three	
Alliteration	
The short last line	
The effect of the rhyme	

The question students will have to complete in the examination (Section A of Unit 2: poetry across time) will be something like Task D.

Task D

How does Nichols present the effects of the hurricane and its effects upon her? *(24 marks)*

Now **compare** how the effects of nature on man are shown in one other poem from the section you have read. *(12 marks)*

You can see that the notes that you have produced would provide a good basis for these answers. This is a 45-minute answer, so 30 minutes should be spent on (a) and 15 minutes on (b).

The word **compare** is emboldened, so it is not a polite request: it is an imperative. In other words, you have to do it.

We have already seen answers to the first part of this question, but now prepare an answer for part (b) by copying out and filling in the following table. You need only find one point of comparison for each box: you only have 15 minutes to answer this question.

Focus	Hurricane Hits England	Patrolling Barnegat
Meaning (what the poet is 'on about')	Nichols is writing about…	Similarly, Whitman is…
Language	Point: Nichols uses some African Caribbean Example: '… Explain: In order to…	On the other hand, Whitman's most obvious device is… I think he does this to…
Structure	Lots of short lines	Whitman's poem is very different
Form (or way of doing something: its shape or arrangement)	Lots of examples in a story-like (narrative) structure	In contrast, Whitman's poem is… He does this to…

Student response to Task D

Both poets are ostensibly writing about the effects of nature on man, but they are, in my opinion, doing this for different reasons. Whereas Nichols is writing about the effects of the hurricane on Britain, she is really writing about a more profound effect on her psyche as this force of nature links the triangular trade routs in its ferocity: 'Like some dark ancestral spectre', which she eventually identifies with when she screams:

'I am aligning myself to you,

I am following the movement of your winds'

Whitman is also ostensibly writing about the effects of a 'wild' and 'roaring' gale on man. However, he is striving to convey a sense of mystery and terror as he describes 'That savage trinity warily watching' and his nature is not comforting in any way.

Both poets use repetition to help to present their ideas. Nichols repeats the names of the hurricane in the different cultures almost as if it were a chant or prayer. This repetition is even more noticeable in Whitman's poem where he repeats the same '-ing' present participle, or gerund, at the end of every line. This again gives the feeling of a prayer, but it also makes the poem even more scary, almost like a witch's chant.

The structure and form of the two poems is very different, with Nichols using the number of short lines to slow the reader down and make them think. Whitman's poem is more solid and linear with its continuous nature continuing until the last line, which is shorter and makes the reader think. 'That savage trinity warily watching' is almost like the trinity of 'Huracan, Oya and Shango' in Nichols' poem.

Examiner's comment

Although the student runs out of steam in the last paragraph, it is almost as if she can't wait to convey that last imaginative and insightful comparison which places this answer in the 'A' band of marks. There is a consistent comparison throughout, based on the Assessment Objectives, and an integrated use of exemplification throughout.

However, it is that last sentence which lifts this response and it is the planning process that gave the student the eventual insight. The mark scheme for A grades states: 'Candidates make illuminating connections and comparisons between texts.' This is such an illuminating connection, which nearly always appears near the end of a response when a candidate has 'warmed up' and written the answers that examiners are almost expecting. This sort of answer only comes when you are 'developing and sustaining'.

> **Remember:** try to integrate your quotations within your answer. If you can make the references look like extensions of your own writing/ thoughts then that is what the examiner wants.

Note the importance of form. The candidate above never mentions that Whitman's poem is 14 lines long, because it is not really a sonnet, but you should be aware that if a poet chooses to write in the sonnet form, then it has been done for a reason. See page 166 for more on sonnets and the importance of their form.

Finally, this book is all about transferable skills and comparison is a transferable reading skill between English, English Language and English Literature.

Assessment for Learning

Look at the *Chat* and *Coarse Fishing* magazine covers from earlier in the book.

In groups, discuss the similarities and differences between these two front pages, focusing on the:

- language
- structure
- form

These two texts could be read as poems, in the way that the Sabine Lebrun article is looked at for its 'poetic' qualities (or otherwise) elsewhere in the book. You are now going to make comparisons between the two texts used for assessment of 'English' by using the Assessment Objectives for English Literature. English Literature requires students to make comparisons and explain links between texts, evaluating writers' different ways of expressing meaning and achieving effects.

D
Literature

Chapter 9

Unseen poetry

Where is this assessed?

This is assessed in Unit 2 (Section B: responding to an unseen poem).

How is this assessed?

This will be assessed via one 30-minute question on an unseen poem as part of the externally assessed Unit 2: poetry across time. There will be a two-part question that will include:

- what the poet is saying
- how the poet is saying it

There will be 18 marks for this question, which translates to 12% of your overall English Literature mark: this is not quite as important as other aspects of the externally assessed units, but it is basically worth more than a grade, so it needs to be addressed in some detail.

Your answer will be mainly assessed via the first two Assessment Objectives. As with previous aspects of any reading assessment it is not assessed by asking you to tell the story, so you are not going to get told the story of any text in this section.

You are going to be asked to:

- respond to texts critically and imaginatively; select and evaluate relevant textual detail to illustrate and support interpretations
- explain how language, structure and form contribute to writers' presentation of ideas, themes and settings
- evaluate writers' different ways of expressing meaning and achieving effects. This will not be assessed because there is no comparative aspect
- possibly, evaluate how the poem relates texts to their social, cultural and historical contexts; explain how texts have been influential and significant to self and other readers in different contexts and at different times

Grade A	Confident and enthusiastic response that evaluates writers' choices using apt textual references.
Grade C	Clear understanding and demonstration of how writers use ideas and themes to affect the reader with reference to textual detail.
Grade F	Involved and personal responses to language effects with reference to significant details.

Key words	What the key words mean
conceptualisation	The 'big idea' that a writer has when planning to write a text. As long as you are able to find evidence to back up your view, your view of the 'big idea' may differ from the writer's. The main issue is: is there textual evidence to support your view?
connotation	The connotations of a word are its associations, or overtones. They can be as important as its primary meaning. It is often possible to group the connotations of words in a poem, for example, positive, negative or neutral associations. The 'weighting' of the words can reveal a lot about the mood of the text.
evaluates	Puts a value on something in relation to something else or gives an opinion about something's relative worth.
references	You do not necessarily have to include quotations: references to line number or the position within a text can suffice.
unseen	You will not have had any access to this poem before the examination, but you do know what the Assessment Objectives are.

Unseen poems are the same as the unseen element in the reading section of Unit 1 in English and English Language. It is nothing to be frightened of if you remember that your answer will be marked by the same Assessment Objectives as for everything else in English, English Language and English Literature.

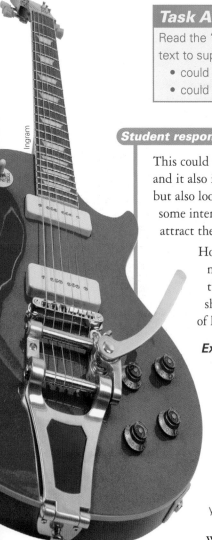

We will start with something we have already read and studied, but for the purpose of reading in English and English Language.

Look at the 'Possible punk princess?' article on page 6. This is not a poem, but it is a text with:

- imagery
- some linguistic devices
- structural devices
- form

> **Task A**
>
> Read the 'Possible punk princess?' article on page 6. Use evidence from the text to support a view that this:
> - could be a poem
> - could be something other than a poem

Student response to Task A

This could well be a poem because there is a vivid image that attracts the reader and it also illustrates the main point of the article because she looks like a punk, but also looks a bit dull and worn out. It could also be a poem because there is some interesting use of language, like the alliterative title, which would help to attract the reader to the article in the first place.

However, it is not really a poem because it is written in paragraphs and not stanzas, which means that the line breaks are decided randomly and they do not really enhance the meaning of the text: they do not give shape and structure. Also, there is not enough evidence of the careful use of language that you would expect in a poem.

Examiner's comment

This response clearly answers the question and uses evidence from the text to support the student's views. This fulfils all of the criteria for C and is working towards a B response.

How to improve

To get that B you really need to develop points and go beyond a simple and structured response to the question. 'Identifying and commenting' will get you a C grade, but you need to aim for a B in order to ensure your grade. You may not always be 'original' and 'illuminating' (Grade A descriptors) but you have to 'generally attempt' these skills.

We will look now at some short poems. Note that 'short' does not necessarily mean 'easy'.

Fog

The fog comes
on little cat feet.
It sits looking
over harbour and city
on silent haunches
and then moves on.

Carl Sandburg

Ingram

Task B

Read this poem and
explain what you
think it is saying
about fog.

Note: This sort of question will always refer to the first
Assessment Objective:

'Respond to texts critically and imaginatively; select
and evaluate relevant textual detail to illustrate and
support interpretations.'

Student response to Task B

The poet seems to be saying that fog is not an obvious phenomenon, but one that
seems to creep surreptitiously, like a cat. In fact, it is not 'like' a cat: it is a cat.
The metaphor conveys the strength of the image as the fog envelops the city.

There are only 21 words in this poem, so each one has to count. For example,
most of the lines begin with prepositions or 'and' so there is a seamless flow from
beginning to end. However, this flow is slow and sinuous, like a cat 'on silent
haunches'.

Examiner's comment

This clearly fulfils all of the aspects of the Assessment Objective, but never really develops any point. In order to improve, the student needs to 'develop and sustain' a point in order to show evidence of the necessary evaluation mentioned in the Assessment Objective. The student also begins to answer the second part of the question and would not gain any marks for bringing in extraneous material. This is simply a 'what' question and students must save the 'how' for the second part of the question. This is not really an exam answer, so has not been awarded a grade.

Assessment for Learning

Identify where this student has actually used evidence from the poem to back up his views. Discuss with a partner whether this exemplification is always successful.

Task C

How does the poet use the metaphor of a cat in this poem?

Note: This sort of question will refer to the second Assessment Objective:

'Explain how language, structure and form contribute to writers' presentation of ideas, themes and settings).'

Student response to Task C

A metaphor is a very strong literary device, which is necessary in this poem because it is so short and the device has to make an effect in a relatively short space. In my opinion, this is certainly the case.

The cat is anthropomorphised so that it becomes an almost malevolent creature 'looking over city and harbour' with the slow rhythm of the poem adding to the sense of menace.

On the other hand, the metaphor is softened by the choice of adjectives, like 'little' and 'silent' which make the cat less of a threat. The image is very visual and succeeds in making the reader link aspects of 'fog' with certain aspects of 'cats', like the manner in which they wrap themselves around things with their sinuous nature.

Examiner's comment

This is more detailed and 'begins to' develop and sustaina response with some tentative imagination in the final paragraph of the answer. The answer is working towards a B response and would require greater leaps of imagination and more evaluation in order to gain an A grade.

Task D

Read the following poem and explain what you think the poet is saying about the eagle:

The Eagle

He clasps the crag with crooked hands;
Close to the sun in lonely lands,
Ring'd with the azure world he stands.

The wrinkled sea beneath him crawls;
He watches from his mountain walls,
And like a thunderbolt he falls.

Alfred, Lord Tennyson

Hemera Technologies

Student response to Task D

In my opinion, the poet is in awe of eagles. There are several words in the poem that communicate this 'shock and awe': 'He', 'world' and 'thunderbolt'. I will develop my views on the uses of poetic devices in the second part of the response, but I think that the poet is saying that this is a mighty and awesome creature. The personification (which I will look at in more detail later) gives the eagle an almost mythical, god-like stature and this is emphasised by its description as being 'like a thunderbolt'.

The poet leaves us in no doubt with its lofty eerie over-looking the world, with its almost flimsy 'wrinkled sea' which appears so tiny from his lofty perch. The use of the pronoun 'He' stresses the human, almost god-like, stature of this creature. No wonder eagles are so often used as symbols of national prowess on flags and insignia (e.g. America).

Examiner's comment

These are notes towards an examination answer, but they clearly show that the student is willing to make leaps of imagination to explain the 'what' of this question. Also, the student clearly grasps that the 'how' of the question should all be left to the second part.

How to improve

Knowing what not to write in an answer is often as important as knowing what to write. It is not possible to carry marks over from one part of an answer to another, so you must clearly answer the question in front of you, then develop that answer for a better mark.

Task E

How does the poet use poetic devices in this poem?

Copy out and complete the following table, part of which has been completed for you already.

Poetic device	Example	Effect
Personification	'He clasps...'	To give the eagle human and god-like qualities and to make the reader even more awed, but able to empathise in some way
Alliteration	'clasps the crag... ...crooked... ...close...crawls'	
Simile		
Rhyme		
Rhythm		

Task F

Choose one of the poetic devices used and 'sustain and develop' your notes from above into an examination response. You should aim to write about half a side by 'writing a lot about a little'.

Remember: write about the blindingly obvious points first and pick up on any other obvious devices. That is what the examiner will expect. Examiners want to reward you, not to punish you.

Student response to Task F

I have chosen the second poetic device, alliteration, because it is so noticeable and accounts for so many words in what is a relatively short poem. Approximately 20% of the words are alliterative, so the poet certainly wanted to draw the reader's attention to some aspect of the eagle's nature.

The alliterative consonant 'c' is hard and connotes well with the harsh landscape in which the eagle lives and Tennyson accentuates this harshness by linking the landscape with the sharp and vicious nature of its 'crooked hand'. Why 'hand', why not 'claw'? Tennyson has made a conscious decision to continue the personification into this image, but he also he does not want the alliteration to be so invasive as to appear childish and immature. Had he used the word 'claw' it might have diminished the overall effect of the alliteration by making the poem too much like a child's rhyme. The poem already rhymes in a very definite manner, so I think that he did not want to gamble with an over-use of alliteration. 'He' and 'hands' at opposite ends of the first line of the poem continue the personification and have a hint of alliteration in them as well.

However, I must personally conclude that I believe that the choice of the word 'hands' was also prompted by the poet having to find a rhyme with the word 'lands': a sure reason in my mind for not including rhyme in poetry.

Examiner's comment

This is a grade-A response. Look in the Assessment for Learning that follows for all of the descriptors for this grade. You will find that this student's response gives examples of each, without the response being very long. The student has kept a clear view of the task and has a good knowledge of the skills required for higher grade performance. The comments on hands vs claws and the response to the use of rhyme exemplify the sparky, individualistic responses of students at this level. There is also a personal aspect to this answer in the final paragraph which exemplifies the descriptor which states that students should: 'confidently explore' and 'convey ideas persuasively and cogently.'

Assessment for Learning

Find evidence of performance in the following Grade A descriptors in the above answer:

- enthusiasm
- critical response
- confident exploration of how language, structure and form contribute to meaning
- how Tennyson achieves effects on the reader (or not)
- making illuminating connections
- the impact of historical contexts
- conveying ideas persuasively
- supporting ideas with apt textual references

The following poem is much longer, but it is no harder. Read it for the first time with the last word of ten of the lines missing.

Timothy Winters

Timothy Winters comes to school
With eyes as wide as a football-pool,
Ears like bombs and teeth like;
A blitz of a boy is Timothy Winters.

up

His belly is white, his neck is dark
And his hair is an exclamation mark.
His clothes are enough to scare a crow
And through his britches the blue winds blow.

bombardier

When teacher talks he won't hear a
And he shoots down dead the arithmetic bird,
He licks the pattern off his
And he's never even heard of the Welfare State.

ten

word

Timothy Winters has bloody
And he lives in a house on Suez Street,
He sleeps in a sack on the kitchen floor
And they say there aren't boys like him any more.

gin

splinters

Old Man Winters likes his beer
And his missus ran off with a
Grandma sits in the grate with a
And Timothy's dosed with an.

The Welfare Worker lies awake
But the law's as tricky as a ten-foot snake,
So Timothy Winters drinks his cup
And slowly goes on growing.

feet

plate

At morning Prayers the Master
For children less fortunate than ourselves,
And the loudest response in the room is when
Timothy Winters roars 'Amen!'

helves

So come one angel, come on
Timothy Winters says 'Amen
Amen amen amen amen.'
Timothy Winters, Lord.
Amen.

aspirin

Charles Causley

Task G

Working with a partner, decide where these words fit in the poem. They are all final, rhyming words in a line and they are not in the order that they appear in the poem:

bombardier,	helves
ten:	feet
word	aspirin
gin	plate
splinters	up

Task H

What do you think the poem is saying about boys like Timothy Winters?

A social worker might visit the Winters' house to assess whether Timothy needs to be taken into care. Write the social worker's report after having visited Timothy's house.

Note: This sort of task is never going to appear in the English Literature examination, but it is exactly the sort of thing that students may be required to do in the 'Recreation' part of English Controlled Assessment Unit 3. 'Recreation' is one of the tasks students might choose in addition to the 'Moving Images' unit, which is compulsory.

Student response to Task H

It is difficult to remain professional under such circumstances, but I would advise that Timothy Winters would be better cared for if he were not living with his father and grandmother in Suez Street.

When I arrived, Timothy was in a dazed state sitting by the fire, almost as if he were under the influence of drugs. I also have reason to believe that Timothy has no bed of his own, but sleeps like a dog in a sack on the floor.

There was, however, no doubt about the grandmother. Several empty gin bottles littered the floor and she was abusive and difficult to communicate with. I was concerned that she might set herself alight because she was so close to the fire. There was, according to the grandmother, no evidence of Mrs Winters returning in view of the state of the house and her relationship with an RAF bombardier. Mr Winters was, according to his mother, 'getting slavvered' in the Dog and Bone.

The following day I visited Timothy's school where I watched him during an arithmetic lesson. He had no concept of addition or subtraction, but he was well-mannered and grateful for the little support he was receiving. His teachers reported that he never complained and was the most vociferous when saying prayers of thanks in assembly.

I slept little last night worrying and wondering about what could be done to help Timothy. There is no evidence of physical abuse, apart from the possible use of drugs, but his clothes are a source of bullying in school. He has large rips in his trousers and he smells. In addition, his teeth are in a very poor state and he has never been to the hairdressers.

As I mentioned at the outset, Timothy Winters needs to be taken into care, but we all know how slippery the law is. I just hope that we are not too late to help this young man for whom nothing seems to be going right.

Sonnets

When a poet chooses to write a 14-line poem, then it is more than likely that he or she is:

- writing a poem that has connotations of love poems or sonnets from the English Literary Heritage
- writing a poem that willfully contradicts this archetypally idealistic form of love poem

Sonnets usually utilise the 14 lines as a vehicle for dialectic (to convey a logical argument) or a particular view of a matter. The three quatrains develop different aspects of the argument or view and the couplet at the end usually clinches the argument or underlines the view. A good example of a modern sonnet might be Simon Armitage's 'Poem'. You need to know this if you are going to write meaningfully about the choice of this form.

Many poets write sonnets, with the most famous being Shakespeare and Donne. However, we are going to look at two poets who subvert this form for their own needs.

Task A

Read the following poem and discuss with a group of fellow students the different aspects of the form and structure of this poem. Make notes on the following:

- the rhyme, or pararhyme and its effect on the reader
- the different stanza form
- the effect of 'The kind old sun...'
- the poet's purpose in writing this poem

Illustrated London News

Futility

Move him into the sun —
Gently its touch awoke him once,
At home, whispering of fields unsown.
Always it woke him, even in France,
Until this morning and this snow.
If anything might rouse him now
The kind old sun will know.

Think how it wakes the seeds, —
Woke, once, the clays of a cold star.
Are limbs, so dear-achieved, are sides,
Full-nerved, — still warm, — too hard to stir?
Was it for this the clay grew tall?
— O what made fatuous sunbeams toil
To break earth's sleep at all?

Wilfred Owen

> **Remember:** look at form/shape before you start actually reading. Then look for rhyme, line length, lots of words on one subject or of one type (semantic field).

Task B

How does the poet subvert (or use for his own purposes) the form of the sonnet in this poem?

Student response to Task B

Sonnets are usually love poems, but this poem is a frustrated and heart-felt plea to stop the war that was killing so many young men:

'Are limbs, so dear-achieved, are sides,
Full-nerved, — still warm, — too hard to stir?
Was it for this the clay grew tall?'

This is a long quotation, but it encapsulates the feelings of the poet. The sonnet form does not allow for any wasted words and the pararhyme, or almost rhyme, keeps the reader focused on the horror of the events on this field of death where the sun can no longer awaken him. The sunbeams are 'fatuous' and useless in their efforts and there is no more love in this world.

Assessment for Learning

With the same group of students, read this response and discuss whether you agree with what the student is writing.

Task C

Now read this famous poem by Christina Rossetti. This poem is often read out at funerals.

Sonnet

Remember me when I am gone away,
Gone far away into the silent land;
When you can no more hold me by the hand,
Nor I half turn to go yet turning stay.
Remember me when no more, day by day,
You tell me of our future that you plann'd:
Only remember me; you understand
It will be late to counsel then or pray.
Yet if you should forget me for a while
And afterwards remember, do not grieve:
For if the darkness and corruption leave
A vestige of the thoughts that once I had,
Better by far you should forget and smile
Than that you should remember and be sad.

Christina Rossetti

Task D

What do you think the poet is saying about dying?

How does the poet use the form of the sonnet in the poem?

Christina Rossetti is writing in the form of a love poem, but is writing that those who love her should remember her gladly and not sadly. She wants those who love her to get on with their lives when she is gone, as she states in the first line and repeats. She just wants those who love her to remember her and not to grieve, but 'Better by far you should forget and smile' and get on with their lives and the future that was planned.

It is not, however, a love poem. The line: 'You tell me of our future that you plann'd' hints that at least one of those who loved her was a bit of a control freak, trying to plan her future for her.

As mentioned at the outset, Rossetti is writing in the form of a sonnet with a very intricate rhyme scheme: abbaabbacddece (as highlighted). This intricate rhyme scheme draws attention to the last word in every line and thereby links the ideas between one line and another. For example: 'away', 'stay', 'day', 'pray' link an important underlying concept of remembrance and prayer that should be remembered. The last word in the poem is 'sad', which sort of contradicts the obvious meaning. Although the poet is saying that those who remember should not be sad, it could be read that the reader 'should remember and be sad'. The last word is emphasised and carries the whole weight of the very structured form.

So this poem has a sting in the tail, in my opinion. The sonnet form suggests a love poem, but this poem would leave those that loved her wondering, so I really think that the poet is saying: do not dare to forget me and my death is partly your fault for being so controlling: 'It will be late to counsel then or pray.'

Examiner's comment

There is a real sense that this student is 'enthusiastically and critically' (grade-A descriptors) exploring how the form of this poem contributes to the poet's varied ways of presenting her ideas. There is a persuasive tone throughout and plenty of textual evidence to support the student's views. There is also a clear identification of the social, historical and cultural aspects of the poem with the student beginning to come to terms with how form contributes to meaning and even the subversion of that form.

This is working towards an A grade.

Positive and negative connotation

You might have noticed that some of the words in 'The Tyger' on page 136 have positive connotations (e.g. 'bright') whereas others have decidedly negative connotations (e.g. 'tears'). Sorting words according to whether they have positive or negative connotations can be helpful when you are making sense of what a writer is trying to do. A piece of writing that contains many positive words might suggest hope, optimism, joy etc. A piece of writing that is full of negative words could suggest gloom, depression, hopelessness etc.

Task A

Read the poem below. It deals with the natural landscape and the writer tries to convey a particular mood by the connotations of the words.

> 'Twas one of those dark, cloudy days
> That sometimes come in summer's blaze,
> When heaven drops not, when earth is still,
> And deeper green is on the hill.
> Lonely at her window sitting,
> While the evening stole away;
> Fitful winds, foreboding, flitting
> Through a sky of cloudy grey.
> There are two trees in a lonely field;
> They breathe a spell to me;
> A dreary thought their dark boughs yield,
> All waving solemnly.

> *Untitled, Emily Brontë (1838)*

Task B

Copy out the following table and fill it in. It has been started for you.

Positive connotations	Negative connotations
blaze	dark
deeper green	cloudy

Task C

Think about the connotations of the words the poet uses and write a few sentences on this poem, commenting on the feelings that each poet is trying to convey.

Student response to Task C

The poet uses a lot of negative connotations and so wants to make the reader feel sad. There are some happy words in the poem, but they just add to the sadness of the poem.

> **Remember:** write down what *you* think the connotations are. It is all right to think differently from everyone else so long as you can support your view by referring to the poem.

Examiner's comment

This response, in note form, is a basic response that simply identifies the words and gives a simple connotation.

To improve, the student needs to go into more detail and to think about the 'associations, or overtones'. The next question demands such a response.

Task D

Re-read lines 9–13 of the poem and comment on the connotations of the image of the trees and how they fit in with the overall connotations of the words in the poem.

Student response to Task D

The fact that there are 'two lonely trees' would make the reader believe that the poet wishes them to represent something more than the obvious. The overall negative connotations of most of the words in the poem would lead the reader to believe that the poet is referring to a sad break-up of a relationship. The fact that the trees breathe and wave gives an ephemoral anthropomorphic nature to them and makes them seem to be a symbolic representation of a recent break-up.

Examiner's comment

This is much better. It is not the nature of the vocabulary being used (which tends to be a bit overbearing and pompous), but the way that the student begins to show an understanding that writers' choices of words can enhance the meaning. Another term for this is 'conceptualisation', which is an A* skill.

Task E

Read the following poem and copy out and fill in the table below.

Morning showers

Now the meadow water smokes,
And the hedgerow's dripping oaks
Pitter-patter all around
And dimple the once dusty ground;
The spinners' threads about the weeds
Are hung with little drops in beads;
Clover silver-green becomes,
And purple-blue surrounds the plums,
And every place breathes fresh and fair
When morning pays her visit there.
The waterfowl with suthering wing
Dive down the river, splash and spring
Up to the very clouds again
That sprinkle scuds of coming rain,
That fly and drizzle all the day
Till dripping grass is turned to grey;
The various clouds now move or lie
Like mighty travellers in the sky,
All mountainous and ridged and curled,
That may have travelled round the world.

John Clare (1825)

Positive connotations	Negative connotations	Neutral connotaions

Task F

How do the connotations link with the poet's use of rhyme and rhythm to convey a particular mood?

Student response to Task F

This is a pre-1914 poem and the poet has used a definite rhyme scheme to help to convey the overall mood in the poem. The overall mood is melancholy with the pathetic fallacy of the dull and drizzly weather according with the poet's overall feelings.

The most obvious place where the poet links connotations of words and rhyme is the end of the poem:

'The various clouds now move or lie

Like mighty travellers in the sky,

All mountainous and ridged and curled,

That may have travelled round the world.'

This is a long quotation, but it amply shows how the connotations of dampness and the 'drizzly' nature of the weather somehow reflect the poet's feelings. This is further accentuated by the rhyme scheme, which gives an inevitability to the poem and to the poet's sadness. There is an example of personification to render the clouds even more threatening and sad for the poet.

Examiner's comment

This is of a similar level of performance to the former response with the student beginning to tease out meanings by focusing on small excerpts from the poem, which give a key, or way into the poem. The quotation, as the student already knows, is too long and overpowers the rest of the answer.

It is not only poets that use connotation. In the prose passage below the author describes an airfield in the opening of a novel.

The Looking Glass War

Snow covered the airfield.

It had come in from the north, in the mist, driven by the night wind, smelling of the sea. There it would stay all winter, threadbare on the grey earth, an icy, sharp dust; not thawing and freezing, but static like a year without seasons. The changing mist, like the smoke of war, would hang over it, swallow up now a hangar, now the radar hut, now the machines; release them piece by piece, drained of colour, black carrion on a white desert.

John Le Carré (1965)

Section D

Literature

Take the word 'carrion' from the extract. Carrion is dead and rotting flesh. This word alone carries unpleasant connotations that can influence the way you see the whole passage.

Task G

Look at the other connotations in the passage above and say what mood the writer is trying to create.

This is the opening of a spy novel. Can you guess why the author describes the airfield in this way?

Discuss your answer to these questions in a group and prepare some notes in readiness for a class discussion.

Glossary

Throughout the English, English Language and English Literature examinations you are required to appreciate and discuss how writers use language to create effects and influence readers. There are a number of terms that are helpful when discussing language and they are defined below.

These terms are a kind of shorthand that will save you from giving lengthy explanations every time a particular language feature appears. They allow you to be more precise in your comments on a writer's language. For example, rather than saying, 'The writer uses a lot of descriptive language', you might say, 'The writer uses a large number of adjectives connected with colour'. However, simply knowing the terms does not necessarily indicate that you understand the language being used, any more than being able to identify a goalkeeper shows you really understand the game of football. In other words, you must be able to explain the effects they are creating. The entries also include some examination and media terms.

Active and passive verbs

We most often use verbs in the **active voice**:

> The dog **bit** the man.

We can turn this sentence into the **passive voice** quite simply:

> The man **was bitten** by the dog.

The passive form is generally regarded as more formal than the active. An important feature of the passive is that it can be *impersonal*, in the sense that it is not necessary to indicate who has performed an action. Watch out for media texts in which the passive is used to conceal the full facts. For example:

Active: The company sacked its staff. (The company is responsible)
Passive: The staff were sacked. (Who is responsible?)

Adjectives

Words such as 'green', 'exciting', 'happy', 'doubtful', 'extended' and 'difficult' are adjectives. Either they come before a noun and add to its sense, as in 'the happy children', or they can be connected with a noun through the verb '**to be**': 'The children were happy'.

The thoughtful use of adjectives can turn a vague statement into something richer and more precise.

Adverbs

Adverbs add information to verbs ('He ran **quickly**') and adjectives ('The music was **unbearably** loud').

Many adjectives can be turned into adverbs by the addition of '–**ly**': sad – sadly; strong – strongly; disappointing – disappointingly; furious – furiously. This is not a universal rule, however; you cannot say 'daftly' or 'greenly'.

Do not overuse adverbs in your writing, even if you can use them accurately. Used sparingly and for effect they can make your writing more sophisticated.

Alliteration

The technique of repeating the initial letter or sound in adjacent words to create an atmospheric or onomatopoeic effect, e.g. 'Degged with dew, dappled with dew'. Alliteration can also link words in the reader's mind to emphasise certain aspects of the sense.

Notice that alliteration is only to do with the sounds. It may draw attention to particular words, but you must be careful not to make exaggerated claims for alliteration, e.g. 'The poet uses alliteration to show he is angry'.

Analysis

Examining texts in detail, passing comment on features such as their construction, the author's methods, the feelings conveyed etc.

Argument

The organisation of information into a clear order that leads towards a conclusion.

Audience

The type of person, or people, you may be writing for.

Communication

The act of sharing or exchanging information.

Conjunctions

Words that link words, phrases or clauses in a sentence, e.g. 'and', 'but', 'therefore'.

Connotation

The connotations of a word are its associations or overtones. They can be as important as its primary meaning. It is often useful to group the connotations of words in a poem, for example, into **positive**, **negative** and **neutral** associations. The 'weighting' of the words can reveal a lot about the overall mood of the text.

Controlled assessment

This replaces coursework from September 2010. It takes place in controlled conditions. However, candidates can prepare for these tasks and can take notes into the controlled assessment sessions which usually last between 3 and 4 hours. It is meant to provide a greater level of control than coursework and aims to develop a fresher response from candidates.

Demarcated

Limits or boundaries are established, usually with punctuation in a sentence, e.g. using a capital letter and full stop.

Dialect

Dialect is a way of speaking usually associated with a region or country. Writers often use dialect forms to lend authenticity to their work. West Indian writers, in particular, use dialect forms to make their work a true reflection of their culture.

Remember that dialect is not incorrect English. It is not Standard English (which itself grew out of a dialect) that has somehow gone wrong.

Direct and indirect speech

Direct speech is the reporting of what someone has said or written by quoting his/her exact words. Indirect speech tries to get over, or convey, what was meant, without repeating the exact words.

Discourse markers

Signposts used in written or formal oral communication. They help to communicate the different stages of a formal speech. In writing, they help a writer to structure a text more meaningfully by using words like: 'First...', 'Second...', 'Furthermore...'.

Discursive

Covering a wide range of subjects and coming to conclusions through reason and not intuition.

Enjamb(e)ment

Sometimes known as 'run-on lines', enjambement describes lines of poetry in which the sense continues from one line to the next without a clear break.

Enjambement generates two sets of meaning:

1 the grammatical sense of the complete sentence
2 the sense created by each individual line

Evaluation

Looking at a text and considering its value or worth. When you are asked to evaluate the effectiveness of a piece of writing you must consider the impact the piece might have on the reader.

Figure of speech

A use of words that diverges from its normal meaning, e.g. 'it's raining cats and dogs.' It can also be a phrase with a specialised meaning not based on its literal meaning, such as a simile, metaphor or personification.

Flier

A short piece of printed material that is widely distributed.

Font

A full set of printing type or screen characters of the same design, e.g. Times New Roman, Arial.

Genre

A type or form with identifiable characteristics. In writing this could mean a leaflet, a letter, an article etc. In film, genre could refer to horror films, action adventures etc.

Hyperbole

Deliberate exaggeration for effect. Hyperbole is widely used in advertising, e.g. 'the **ultimate** garden hose'.

Imagery

Descriptive language in a work of literature that appeals to the senses.

Integrated comment

A quotation or reference that forms part of a sentence (often by being placed, or embedded, in it) and is not on a separate line.

Interpretations

Different ways of reading and explaining a text. Texts often have more than one interpretation.

Intensifiers

Adjectives used to amplify the effect of a word, e.g. '**very** interesting'.

Juxtaposition

Placing two or more words/phrases/images etc. side by side for (ironic) contrast.

Kicker

A newspaper or magazine story designed to stand out from the rest of the page.

Layout

The general appearance and design of the text and images on a page.

Line grammar

The way in which lines of poetry divide up the sense of what is said. Poetry is written in lines that might not always correspond with the usual grammatical sense. The opening and closing words of a line tend to be particularly important because they stand out and attract the reader's attention.

Linguistics

The scientific study of language.

Literal meaning

The word-for-word meaning, which takes no account of implied or wider meanings. For example, 'The bed is lifting out of its nightmares' cannot literally be true, so the poet must be suggesting something entirely different. You usually have to look beyond the literal meaning of the words on the page.

Beware of using 'literally' simply to give emphasis. Don't say 'I was literally drowned on the way to school this morning' when you really mean you got very wet.

Logo

A design used by an organisation that acts like an emblem.

Mark band

A group of marks that cover the top and bottom of a grade on an examination paper.

Mark scheme

The document examiners use to mark candidates' scripts to the same standard.

Media

Any means of mass communication, including film, newspapers, adverts etc.

Media terminology

The words used to describe the features of media texts.

Metaphor and simile

Both these figures of speech use **comparisons** to make an idea more vivid. Metaphor and simile are often referred to as **imagery**.

Metaphor involves an unstated comparison and is a natural part of our language. We use metaphors all the time without really noticing, as in 'The footballer **smashed home** a goal' (obviously nothing is actually smashed).

Simile involves a more direct comparison and is identified by the use of 'like' or 'as'. Like metaphors, similes are often used in everyday speech, e.g. 'The class rushed **like a herd of elephants.**'

Non-fiction
Writing consisting of factual information and ideas.

Onomatopoeia
Words that imitate the sound being described, e.g. 'crackle', 'moan', 'sizzle'. Writers certainly attempt onomatopoeic effects, as in Tennyson's reference to 'The murmuring of innumerable bees', but you should be careful not to think that every use of a word connected with sound is an example of onomatopoeia. Besides, few words actually imitate a sound.

Organisational devices
Features such as paragraphs and columns.

Oxymoron
Using two terms together that normally contradict each other, e.g. 'bitter-sweet'.

Paraphrasing
Restating something in your own words.

Participles
Participles are forms of verbs and are made in two ways from a basic verb. There are two types of participle: **present** and **past**.

> Verb: shout
> Present participle: shouting
> Past participle: shouted

The present participle can suggest continuous action and, skilfully used, can build up a sense of excitement.

Personification
Giving human qualities to inanimate objects, animals or natural phenomena.

Persuading
Trying to make someone think or do something.

Point of view
This term has two senses:

1 an opinion on a subject or an attitude towards something, usually in contrast with another opinion

2 the position of a narrator; e.g. 'My Last Duchess' is written by Browning but the tale is told from the point of view of the Duke of Ferrara

Presentational devices

Visual features, such as bullet points, bold, italics, that are used to make writing more accessible to the reader.

Purpose

The reason why a particular text has been written in the first place.

Repetition

Repetition occurs in all kinds of writing. It can take a number of forms and has various effects. Most obviously, it can be used for **emphasis**, but it may also establish a **pattern**.

Rhetorical question

A question that presumes only one response, so it does not require an answer. Rhetorical questions can be used as a means of drawing your audience in and getting it on your side, e.g. 'Who could refuse someone who has been through such a terrible ordeal?'

Rhyme

Rhyme is probably the most familiar feature of poetry, although not all poetry uses rhyme.

The most common type is **end-rhyme**, in which the last words in lines of poetry have matching sounds, but rhymes can also occur within lines. Poems often have distinctive **rhyme schemes**, so that there is a regular pattern of rhyming syllables. There are innumerable possible rhyming patterns, and some specific forms of poetry, such as the **sonnet**, have strict rhyme schemes.

Rhyme can capture our attention in ways that stretch beyond the basic meaning of the words. For the purpose of the examination, it is useful to think about the meaning and force of the words that the rhymes draw to your attention.

Rhythm

Read out any sentence in English and you will see that there is a reasonably regular pattern of stressed and unstressed syllables. Poets organise stresses into conscious patterns. There is a large number of terms for rhythmical patterns in poetry, all with Greek names. The two most common patterns reflect the basic stress patterns of ordinary speech:

iambic: unstressed followed by stressed (~ /) as in exam

trochaic: stressed followed by unstressed (/ ~) as in English

In traditional poetry it is often easy to recognise a regular pattern of stresses. Much modern poetry uses a more flexible approach, often closer to natural speech, and the rhythm is more of a pulse than a regular pattern. For the purpose of the examination it is best to concentrate on spotting the *main* stresses, especially where they strongly emphasise the sense.

Rule of three

This is based on the fact that lists of three things are more powerful and easier to remember than lists of two or four things. It is a technique used a lot in oratory, for example the speeches of Barack Obama. A famous example is Tony Blair's promise that a Labour government would prioritise 'Education, education, education'.

Setting

The place or situation that forms the background to a piece of narrative. This might give you clues about the wider meaning of the text.

Sonnet

A sonnet is a poem of 14 lines with a strict pattern of rhyme and rhythm. For the reader, the rules are less important than the way the ideas are set out. There are slightly different forms of sonnet but they share a similar *concentrated* three-part thought structure:

1 key idea

2 development

3 conclusion, often with a twist or sting in the tail

Standard English

Standard English is difficult to define, but it is the English you would associate with 'educated' speakers and expect to find in newspapers, textbooks, business documents and so on. It is extremely varied, however, and although you may find large differences in the language of the *Sun* compared with *The Times*, for example, they are both written in Standard English.

Standfirst

The introductory paragraph before the start of a feature in a newspaper or magazine.

Structure

Any element of language which gives what you say or write a meaningful 'shape'. Sometimes, language experts use the word 'structure' to refer to 'grammar'.

Subheading

A heading less important than and 'under' the main one.

Symbol(ism)

A symbol is an object, person or event that represents something more than itself. For example, red has come to symbolise danger.

Writers often employ symbolism but it is up to the reader to make the connections, which may be suggestive and vague. Successful use of symbolism should stimulate our imagination and prompt us to think beyond the text's immediate subject matter.

Tone

The kind of voice in which something is written (sarcastic, light-hearted, depressing etc.) The tone of a piece of writing is closely linked to its mood.

Verbs

Words that describe action, such as 'run', 'talk', 'investigate', 'consider' and 'sing' are all verbs. A verb is essential to form a sentence; it cannot be left out. For example, 'The student two gallons a day' does not make sense.

You will come across **minor sentences** that do not contain complete verbs. They are often used in newspaper headlines such as 'MOTORWAY TRAFFIC CHAOS FURY', and writers sometimes use minor sentences for special effect.

Word art

Unusual lettering that is designed to make parts of the text stand out.